Spotter
WILDLIFE

Chapter 1 (Birds) was written by Peter Holden and illustrated by Trevor Boyer.

Chapter 2 (Wild Flowers) was written by Christopher Humphries and illustrated by Hilary Burn.
Additional illustrations are by Christine Howes.

Chapter 3 (Trees) was written by Esmond Harris and illustrated by Annabel Milne and Peter Stebbing.

Chapter 4 (Fishes) was written by Alwyne Wheeler and illustrated by Annabel Milne and Peter Stebbing.

Chapter 5 (The Seashore) was written by Su Swallow and illustrated by John Barber.
Additional illustrations are by Joyce Bee, Trevor Boyer and Christine Howes.

Chapter 6 (Insects) was written by George E. Hyde and Anthony Wootton and illustrated by Joyce Bee and Phil Weare.
Additional illustrations are by Andy Martin.

Chapter 7 (Mammals) was written by Alfred Leutscher and illustrated by Chris Shields.

This edition edited by
Casey Horton

Series Editor
Sue Jacquemier

Designer
Sally Burrough

Assistant Designer
Niki Overy

Cover by
John Barber

Additional illustrations
for this edition by
Andy Martin

First published in 1979 by Usborne Publishing Limited, 20 Garrick Street, London WC2

© 1979 by Usborne Publishing Limited

Printed and bound in Great Britain

The name Usborne and the device 🎈 are Trade Marks of Usborne Publishing Ltd.

The material in this book is also available as eight separate books: *Birds, Wild Flowers, Trees, Fishes, The Seashore, Butterflies, Insects,* and *Animals, Tracks & Signs,* in the *Spotter's Guides* series, published by Usborne Publishing Limited.

THE USBORNE
SPOTTER'S GUIDE TO
WILDLIFE

Contents

Introduction

This book is an identification guide to over 1,000 different species of plants and animals found in Britain and Europe. It is divided into seven chapters and in most cases each chapter is concerned with one group of animals and plants, such as birds, wild flowers, trees and so on. Chapter Five covers the wide range of plant and animal life found on seashores.

At the beginning of each chapter there is a special introduction which explains what the chapter is about and how it is arranged. It also has information that will help you to find and identify the plants and animals.

For each species in the book there is a separate illustration and description. Next to the description there is a blank circle so that you can tick off a species when you have found it.

The glossary on page 333 explains the scientific terms used in the book and the index at the back gives both the common English and Latin names of each species.

The book covers the countries coloured red on the map, and for fishes, all the seas that are shown. Some of the species that are described are very rare or not present in Britain but are common in other European countries.

Studying Wildlife

As you become skilled at identifying the plants and animals that you see you will probably want to know more about them. One of the best ways to begin to add to your knowledge of wildlife is to keep a permanent record of the species you have found. You may like to keep a separate book for each subject, or a nature diary in which you record each outing you make and the things you have observed.

It is often difficult to remember all the details about a species after you have spotted it, so it is best to take a small notebook with you when you go out so that you can jot down notes. It is also helpful to make sketches of plants and animals and take photographs if possible. (You will find helpful tips on photographing wild flowers on page 58.)

The information you gather will help you to identify species which are not in this book. When you are looking up references use the Latin name of the plant or animal, as common names often differ from one area to another. Natural history museums, botanical and zoological gardens may have unusual or rare species you cannot find in your area.

Wildlife habitats

Plants and animals live in a wide variety of habitats. In this book most of the descriptions give the habitat in which each species is usually found. Some of the more common habitats are described below. You will probably find at least one of them in your area. (Seashore habitats are described on page 197.)

Hedgerows

Hedgerows are particularly good places to begin to look for wildlife because they provide homes for many kinds of plants and animals. Old hedgerows usually have at least one kind of mature tree or shrub, such as Oak, Hawthorn or Ash, and climbing plants such as Blackberry, Dog Rose and Greater Bindweed. Look for birds such as the Redwing, Bullfinch and Fieldfare which feed on berries. Small mammals, such as the Wood Mouse, Common Shrew and Bank Vole, and many insects make their homes among the plants.

Some hedgerows are planted near ditches and these are good places to look for plants that prefer moist or wet habitats.

Waste places

Small animals and sturdy plants often live on ground that has been cleared of old buildings and in other places that have been disturbed by man in some way. Plants such as the Rosebay Willowherb, Nettle and Shepherd's Purse are common on waste ground. Look for the Cinnabar Moth on Oxford Ragwort and for Tiger Moths and their larvae on Nettles. Ladybirds, Earwigs and Wasps are other insects to look for. Watch for common town birds such as the Starling, Pigeon and Sparrow, and the Kestrel, which is rarer, but sometimes nests in towns.

Woodlands
The kinds of plants and animals you will find in the woodland habitat will depend very much on the type of wood it is. In **Pinewoods**, few flowering plants grow on the ground because the trees let in very little sunlight. In **Oakwoods**, there is more light and the ground is often thick with leaf-mould, flowers and small trees or shrubs. Look in woods for spring flowers and the insects that are attracted to them. Birds and small mammals inhabit trees that produce nuts and fruits.

Chalk grasslands
Chalk grasslands are open, usually treeless, areas. The plant life is made up of species that can live on light, dry soil. Many of them have colourful flowers; look for Knapweed, Cowslip and Clover. The caterpillars of some moths and butterflies, especially the Chalkhill Blue, feed on grassland plants. Brown Hares are common on grassland and, as earthworms are plentiful, Moles sometimes make their homes here. Birds that prefer open places to wooded areas include the Corn Bunting.

Sandy Heathland
Many heathlands have dry, sandy soil. There are usually only a few different types of plant, such as Heather and Gorse, but these cover wide areas. Heathlands are good places to look for birds; watch for Kestrels, Wheatears on open ground, Linnets among bushes and Nightjars where there are trees or bracken. Other animals to look for are the Small Heath and Grayling butterflies and the Badger, which prefers to dig its set in dry soil.

Freshwater habitats

Lakes, ponds, streams, and **rivers** are the homes of many plants and animals. In still or slow-running water, look for Water Crowfoot, Water-lily and Frogbit, and insects, such as the Water Boatman and Great Diving Beetle, that live in water. Sticklebacks, Minnows and Trout are common freshwater fishes. Moorhens, Mallards and Reed Warblers nest among reeds and other waterside plants. Water meadows and marshes that lie along rivers are good places to look for Willow and Alder.

Uplands

Upland habitats vary from the vast, treeless, open spaces of **moors** to rolling **hills** and bleak, rocky **mountains.** Many of the plants which live in these areas are low-growing species that flower late in the year. Heather and Bilberry are common on both moors and mountains. Trees which grow on hills and mountains include the Rowan, and the Ash, which often forms woods on limestone. Look for Voles, Grouse, Skylarks, and Curlews on moors, Red Deer, Sheep and Stoats on hills and mountain slopes.

Wildlife conservation

Many plants and animals are now very rare and some are extinct because their natural habitats have been disrupted or completely destroyed. Woods and hedgerows have been cut down and ponds and rivers drained or polluted; large areas of countryside have been taken over for factories and housing developments.

Just as serious is the destruction caused by visitors to the countryside who pick and uproot wild flowers and disturb animals' nests and homes. Through carelessness they also cause many of the fires which destroy parts of our commons, heaths and forests every year.

Wildlife conservation is concerned with preserving natural habitats and protecting the wildlife which is a part of them. If habitats disappear, so will the plants and animals that depend on them.

9

In most countries conservationists have established nature reserves and sanctuaries for the protection of endangered species. But as cities and towns continue to spread out into the countryside more and more of our wildlife will be in danger.

The Country Code

Everyone can do something to help conserve the wildlife of town and countryside. The Country Code (listed below) explains how to behave in the country but the rules are just the same for city parks, gardens and commons. Follow it when you go out and make sure other people know about it.

Guard against all risk of fire.
Fasten all gates.
Keep dogs under proper control.
Keep to the paths across farm land.
Avoid damaging fences, hedges and walls.
Leave no litter.
Safeguard water supplies.
Protect wildlife, wild plants and trees.
Go carefully on country roads.
Respect the life of the countryside.

Marshland
Many of our marshlands have been drained to provide land for housing and farming. As a result many marshland animals and plants are now rare.

Further Information

A poster, leaflet and a booklet explaining the Country Code in detail is available from the Publications Officer, the *Countryside Commission* (address: John Dover House, Crescent Place, Cheltenham, Gloucestershire GL50 3RA). If you would like to know more about wildlife conservation, contact the *Nature Conservancy Council* (address: The Librarian, 20 Belgrave Square, London SW1X 8PY).

The *British Trust for Conservation Volunteers* makes it possible for people over 16 years of age to do practical work in the countryside. If you are interested and would like further information, contact the Field Director (address: Zoological Gardens, Regent's Park, London NW1 4RY).

Chapter 1
BIRDS

Introduction to Chapter 1

This chapter will help you to identify over 170 species of birds. Some are very common and you will be able to spot them immediately; others are rarer and you may need to gain some practice in bird-watching and visit different habitats before you find the birds.

The illustrations show the birds perched or in flight, depending on how the bird is most often spotted. Juvenile birds are sometimes shown and there are separate pictures of the females (♀) if they are very different from the males (♂). If a bird's summer and winter plumage are very different, both kinds of plumage are shown.

The description next to each bird tells you where to look for it

Chaffinch

15 cm.

and always refers to Britain unless another area is named. It also gives the bird's size. A bird is measured from the tip of its beak to the tip of its tail, as shown in the diagram.

Birdwatching

The garden is a good place to start watching birds, especially if there is a bird table to attract them, and you will be able to study them at close range from a window. Parks, ponds, rivers, school playing fields and old gravel pits are other places which attract birds.

Binoculars are necessary for identifying birds correctly from a distance and for studying their habits. The best sizes are 8 x 30 or 8 x 40 (never more than 10 x 50).

The shape of a bird in flight and the way it flies help to identify it. Notice whether it flies in a straight line, glides, bounces or hovers. Note the colour of its plumage and any special markings, the shape of the beak, colour of its legs and the shape of its feet. Look for signs of birds' feathers, pellets, cracked nuts, footprints etc. when choosing

a site from which to watch; it is a good idea to build a hide of twigs and leaves near a bird's favourite habitat.

Always approach a bird silently and slowly. Wear soft-soled shoes and dark clothing for camouflage. Disguise your shape against a bush or tree whenever possible and if there is no cover, crawl slowly towards the bird on your elbows and knees. Try to approach the bird downwind.

Although bird song is important for identifying birds it is difficult to describe and is therefore not mentioned much in this chapter. Note as many of the songs as you can while you are birdwatching and try to obtain records and tapes to gain additional knowledge. A catalogue of records is available from the R.S.P.B., The Lodge, Sandy, Bedfordshire.

Shag, Gannet, Cormorant

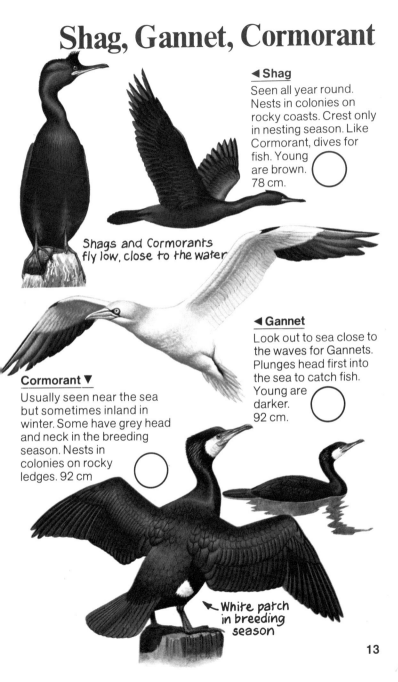

◄ Shag
Seen all year round. Nests in colonies on rocky coasts. Crest only in nesting season. Like Cormorant, dives for fish. Young are brown. 78 cm.

Shags and Cormorants fly low, close to the water

◄ Gannet
Look out to sea close to the waves for Gannets. Plunges head first into the sea to catch fish. Young are darker. 92 cm.

Cormorant ▼
Usually seen near the sea but sometimes inland in winter. Some have grey head and neck in the breeding season. Nests in colonies on rocky ledges. 92 cm

White patch in breeding season

Geese

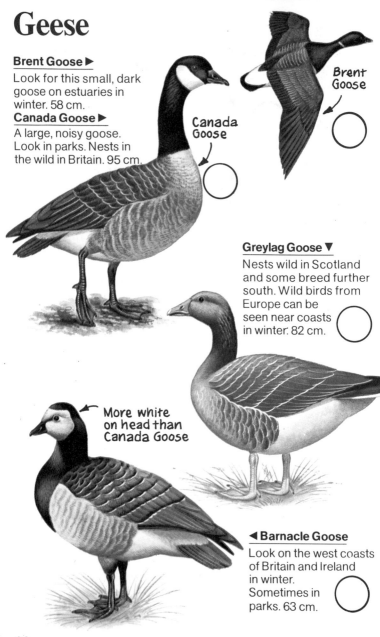

Brent Goose ▶
Look for this small, dark goose on estuaries in winter. 58 cm.

Canada Goose ▶
A large, noisy goose. Look in parks. Nests in the wild in Britain. 95 cm.

Brent Goose

Canada Goose

Greylag Goose ▼
Nests wild in Scotland and some breed further south. Wild birds from Europe can be seen near coasts in winter. 82 cm.

More white on head than Canada Goose

◀ Barnacle Goose
Look on the west coasts of Britain and Ireland in winter. Sometimes in parks. 63 cm.

Geese, Swans

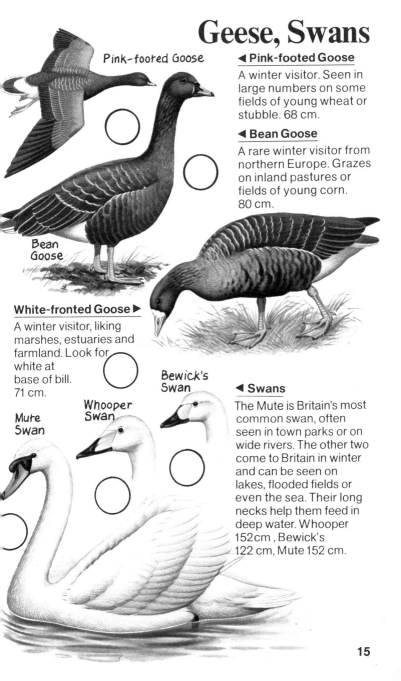

Pink-footed Goose

Bean Goose

White-fronted Goose ▶

A winter visitor, liking marshes, estuaries and farmland. Look for white at base of bill. 71 cm.

Mute Swan

Whooper Swan

Bewick's Swan

◀ Pink-footed Goose

A winter visitor. Seen in large numbers on some fields of young wheat or stubble. 68 cm.

◀ Bean Goose

A rare winter visitor from northern Europe. Grazes on inland pastures or fields of young corn. 80 cm.

◀ Swans

The Mute is Britain's most common swan, often seen in town parks or on wide rivers. The other two come to Britain in winter and can be seen on lakes, flooded fields or even the sea. Their long necks help them feed in deep water. Whooper 152cm , Bewick's 122 cm, Mute 152 cm.

Ducks

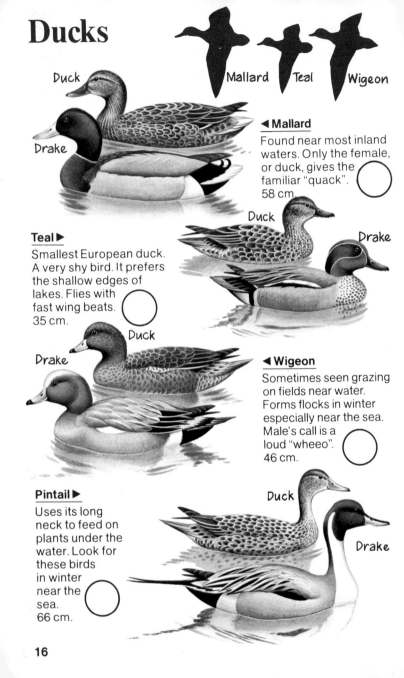

Duck

Drake

Mallard Teal Wigeon

◀ Mallard
Found near most inland waters. Only the female, or duck, gives the familiar "quack".
58 cm.

Duck

Drake

Teal ▶
Smallest European duck. A very shy bird. It prefers the shallow edges of lakes. Flies with fast wing beats.
35 cm.

Duck

Drake

◀ Wigeon
Sometimes seen grazing on fields near water. Forms flocks in winter especially near the sea. Male's call is a loud "wheeo".
46 cm.

Pintail ▶
Uses its long neck to feed on plants under the water. Look for these birds in winter near the sea.
66 cm.

Duck

Drake

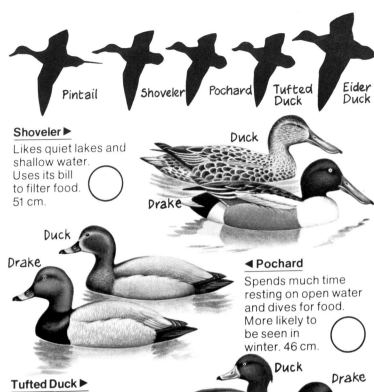

Pintail　Shoveler　Pochard　Tufted Duck　Eider Duck

Shoveler ▶
Likes quiet lakes and
shallow water.
Uses its bill
to filter food.
51 cm.

Duck

Drake

Duck

Drake

◀ Pochard
Spends much time
resting on open water
and dives for food.
More likely to
be seen in
winter. 46 cm.

Tufted Duck ▶
Another diving duck
which is more
common in winter.
Can sometimes
be seen on
town ponds.
43 cm.

Duck

Drake

Duck

Drake

◀ Eider
Breeds around northern
sea shores. We get "eider
down" from its nest. In
eclipse, drakes are
darker with
white wing
patches. 58 cm.

17

Ducks

Goldeneye ▶
A few nest in Scotland, but mainly a winter visitor. Seen on the sea and inland lakes. Often in flocks. Dives frequently. 46 cm.

Duck

Drake

White wing patches in flight

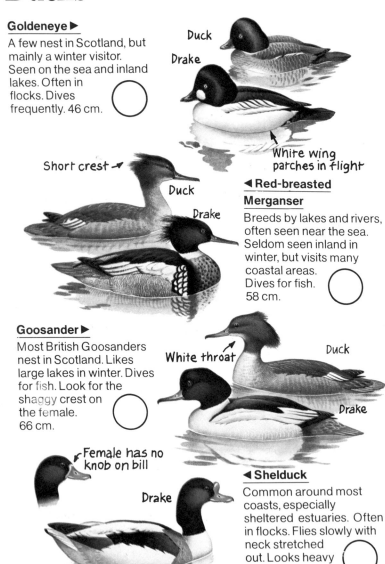

Short crest

Duck

Drake

◀ Red-breasted
Merganser
Breeds by lakes and rivers, often seen near the sea. Seldom seen inland in winter, but visits many coastal areas. Dives for fish. 58 cm.

Goosander ▶
Most British Goosanders nest in Scotland. Likes large lakes in winter. Dives for fish. Look for the shaggy crest on the female. 66 cm.

White throat

Duck

Drake

Female has no knob on bill

Drake

◀ Shelduck
Common around most coasts, especially sheltered estuaries. Often in flocks. Flies slowly with neck stretched out. Looks heavy in flight. 61 cm.

Grebes, Heron, Stork

Great Crested Grebe ▶

Found on inland waters.
Dives for fish. Seldom flies.
Beautiful courtship
displays in spring.
Sometimes seen
on sea in winter.
48 cm.

Crest expands
during display

Winter

Summer

Winter

Summer

◀ Little Grebe or Dabchick

Common on inland waters,
but secretive and
hard to spot. Call is
a shrill trill. 27 cm.

Grey Heron ▶

Usually seen near water.
Nests in colonies in trees.
Eats fish, frogs, small
mammals. Stands
still for long
periods. 92 cm.

Head is drawn
back and legs
stick out
when flying

◀ White Stork

Very rare in Britain. Likes
wet areas. Will nest on
buildings
in Europe.
102 cm.

Birds of Prey

Osprey ▶

Rare summer visitor to
Britain. Some nest
in Scotland. Plunges
into water to catch fish.
Often perches on
dead trees.
56 cm.

Upper parts are
dark brown

◀ **Golden Eagle**

Lives in Scottish Highlands.
Young birds have white on
wings and tail. Glides for
long distances.
Bigger than
Buzzard. 83 cm.

Long broad
wings

Wings narrower
than Buzzard's

Red Kite ▶

This rare bird nests in oak
woods in mid-Wales.
Soars for long
periods. Rare.
62 cm.

Long forked tail

Birds of Prey

Notice the pale wing patches →

◀ Buzzard
A large bird of prey with broad rounded wings. Often seen soaring over moors and farmland as it hunts. Rare in south and eastern England. 54 cm.

♀

Female is larger and browner than male

Sparrowhawk ▶
Broad-winged hawk. Hunts small birds along hedges and woodland edges. Never hovers. Female 38 cm. Male 30 cm.

♂

♀

Long pointed wings and long tail

♂

◀ Kestrel
Well-known for the way it hovers when hunting, especially alongside motorways. Some nest in towns. Eats birds, mammals, insects. 34 cm.

Birds of Prey

Tail shorter and wings longer than Kestrel

◄ Hobby
Catches flying insects and birds in the air. Summer visitor to southern England. Look on heaths and downs. 33 cm.

Peregrine ►
Sea cliffs or inland crags. Hunts over estuaries and marshes in winter. Dives on flying birds at great speed. 38–48 cm.

◄ Goshawk

Looks like a large Sparrowhawk. Lives in dense woods. Rare in Britain. Male 48 cm. Female 58 cm.

Honey Buzzard ►
Summer visitor to British woodlands. Eats mainly grubs of wasps and bees. 51-59 cm.

Rails, Crake

◄ Moorhen
Water bird that lives near ponds, lakes or streams. Unafraid of people in parks, but secretive elsewhere. Juveniles are brown. 33 cm.

Coot ►
Dives a lot. Prefers large lakes. Look for white bill and forehead. Young are grey with pale throats and breasts. Flocks in winter. 38 cm.

◄ Corncrake
Difficult to see as it lives in long grass. Repeats "crex-crex" cry monotonously, especially after dark. Rare in Britain. 27 cm.

Water Rail ►
Secretive bird that lives in reed beds. Listen for its piglet-like squeal. Legs trail in flight. Swims for short distances. 28 cm.

Game Birds

Red Grouse ▶

Willow Grouse ▶

Red Grouse live in
Britain and Ireland,
and Willow Grouse
in northern Europe.
Willow Grouse
is white in
winter.
36 cm.

summer

Willow
Grouse
winter

Red
Grouse

In summer, the
male's plumage is
more brown and
the female's more
yellow than in
autumn

Winter

◀ Ptarmigan

Lives on barren mountain
tops in the north. Has
three different plumages
and is very well
camouflaged.
Allows people to
get close. 34 cm.

Autumn

♀

Female's tail
is forked

♂

Black Grouse ▶

Often found on edge of
moorland, sometimes in
trees, perched or eating
buds. Groups of males
display together
at a lek. Female
41 cm. Male 53 cm.

Male's
tail
curves
outwards

Capercaillie ▶

This large bird lives in coniferous forests in parts of Scotland. Eats pine shoots at tips of branches.
Male 86 cm.
Female 61 cm.

♂

♀

◀ Partridge

Often in small groups. Likes farmland with hedges. Its call is a grating "kirr-ic".
Rarer in Ireland.
30 cm.

Pheasant ▶

Lives on farmland with hedges. Often reared and shot as game. Roosts in trees. Nests on ground. Look for the long tail. Male 87 cm.
Female 58 cm.

♂

Cock Pheasants can vary in colour

♀

◀ Red-legged Partridge

Common in southern and eastern Britain. Fields and open sandy areas. Often runs rather than flies. 34 cm.

Waders

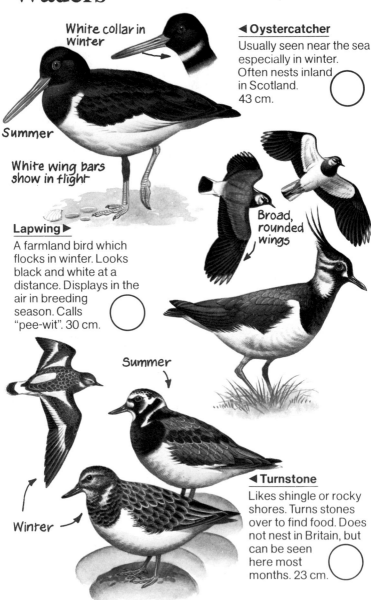

White collar in winter

Summer

White wing bars show in flight

◄ Oystercatcher
Usually seen near the sea especially in winter. Often nests inland in Scotland. 43 cm.

Lapwing ►
A farmland bird which flocks in winter. Looks black and white at a distance. Displays in the air in breeding season. Calls "pee-wit". 30 cm.

Broad, rounded wings

Summer

◄ Turnstone
Likes shingle or rocky shores. Turns stones over to find food. Does not nest in Britain, but can be seen here most months. 23 cm.

Winter

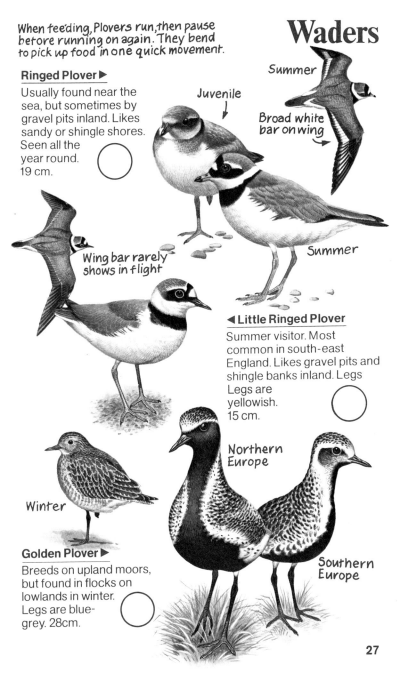

When feeding, Plovers run, then pause before running on again. They bend to pick up food in one quick movement.

Waders

Ringed Plover ▶

Usually found near the sea, but sometimes by gravel pits inland. Likes sandy or shingle shores. Seen all the year round. 19 cm.

Juvenile

Summer

Broad white bar on wing

Summer

Wing bar rarely shows in flight

◀ Little Ringed Plover

Summer visitor. Most common in south-east England. Likes gravel pits and shingle banks inland. Legs Legs are yellowish. 15 cm.

Northern Europe

Winter

Golden Plover ▶

Breeds on upland moors, but found in flocks on lowlands in winter. Legs are blue-grey. 28cm.

Southern Europe

Waders

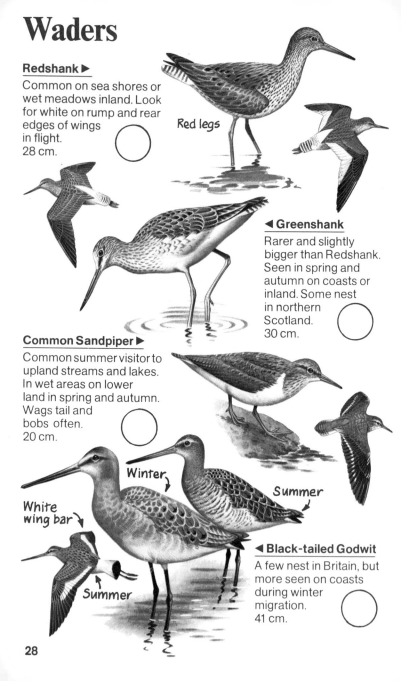

Redshank ▶
Common on sea shores or wet meadows inland. Look for white on rump and rear edges of wings in flight.
28 cm.

Red legs

◀ Greenshank
Rarer and slightly bigger than Redshank. Seen in spring and autumn on coasts or inland. Some nest in northern Scotland.
30 cm.

Common Sandpiper ▶
Common summer visitor to upland streams and lakes. In wet areas on lower land in spring and autumn. Wags tail and bobs often.
20 cm.

White wing bar ↘

Winter ↘

Summer ↘

Summer →

◀ Black-tailed Godwit
A few nest in Britain, but more seen on coasts during winter migration.
41 cm.

Waders

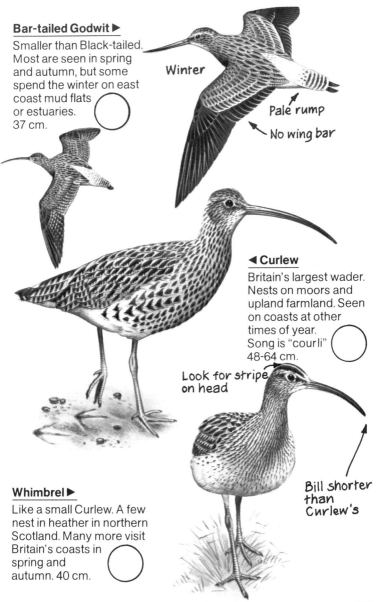

Bar-tailed Godwit ▶
Smaller than Black-tailed.
Most are seen in spring
and autumn, but some
spend the winter on east
coast mud flats
or estuaries.
37 cm.

Winter

Pale rump

No wing bar

◀ Curlew
Britain's largest wader.
Nests on moors and
upland farmland. Seen
on coasts at other
times of year.
Song is "courli"
48-64 cm.

Look for stripe
on head

Bill shorter
than
Curlew's

Whimbrel ▶
Like a small Curlew. A few
nest in heather in northern
Scotland. Many more visit
Britain's coasts in
spring and
autumn. 40 cm.

Waders

◄ Dunlin

A common visitor to sea shores, but nests on moorland in the north. Usually seen in flocks. Beak straight or down-curved. 19 cm.

Winter

Summer

Winter

Knot ►

Seen in huge flocks in winter. Likes sand or mud flats in estuaries. Rare inland. Mainly a winter visitor. Breeds in the Arctic. 25 cm.

◄ Sanderling

Runs back and forth along water's edge on sandy beaches where it catches small animals. Coasts in winter. 20 cm.

Winter

♂ Summer

♀

Ruff ►

Seen in spring and autumn in Britain, but some also winter in wet places. Female 23 cm. Male 29 cm.

Winter ♂

Waders

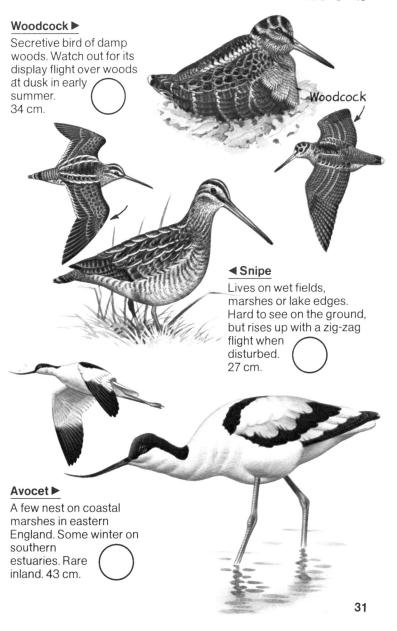

Woodcock ▶
Secretive bird of damp woods. Watch out for its display flight over woods at dusk in early summer.
34 cm.

Woodcock

◀ Snipe
Lives on wet fields, marshes or lake edges. Hard to see on the ground, but rises up with a zig-zag flight when disturbed.
27 cm.

Avocet ▶
A few nest on coastal marshes in eastern England. Some winter on southern estuaries. Rare inland. 43 cm.

Pigeons, Doves

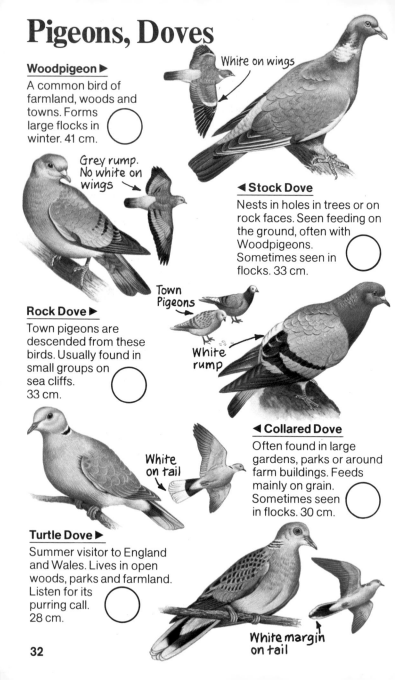

Woodpigeon ▶

A common bird of farmland, woods and towns. Forms large flocks in winter. 41 cm.

White on wings

Grey rump. No white on wings

◀ Stock Dove

Nests in holes in trees or on rock faces. Seen feeding on the ground, often with Woodpigeons. Sometimes seen in flocks. 33 cm.

Rock Dove ▶

Town pigeons are descended from these birds. Usually found in small groups on sea cliffs. 33 cm.

Town Pigeons

White rump

◀ Collared Dove

Often found in large gardens, parks or around farm buildings. Feeds mainly on grain. Sometimes seen in flocks. 30 cm.

White on tail

Turtle Dove ▶

Summer visitor to England and Wales. Lives in open woods, parks and farmland. Listen for its purring call. 28 cm.

White margin on tail

Auks, Fulmar

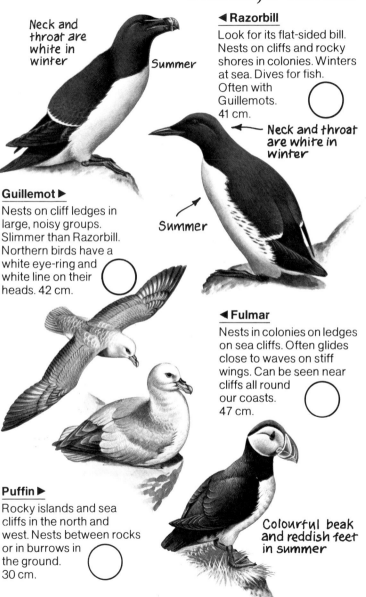

Neck and throat are white in winter

Summer

◀ Razorbill
Look for its flat-sided bill. Nests on cliffs and rocky shores in colonies. Winters at sea. Dives for fish. Often with Guillemots. 41 cm.

Neck and throat are white in winter

Summer

Guillemot ▶
Nests on cliff ledges in large, noisy groups. Slimmer than Razorbill. Northern birds have a white eye-ring and white line on their heads. 42 cm.

◀ Fulmar
Nests in colonies on ledges on sea cliffs. Often glides close to waves on stiff wings. Can be seen near cliffs all round our coasts. 47 cm.

Puffin ▶
Rocky islands and sea cliffs in the north and west. Nests between rocks or in burrows in the ground. 30 cm.

Colourful beak and reddish feet in summer

Gulls

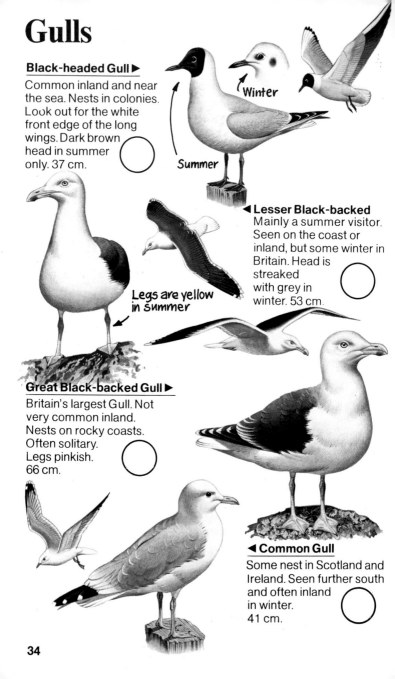

Black-headed Gull ▶

Common inland and near the sea. Nests in colonies. Look out for the white front edge of the long wings. Dark brown head in summer only. 37 cm.

Winter

Summer

◀ Lesser Black-backed

Mainly a summer visitor. Seen on the coast or inland, but some winter in Britain. Head is streaked with grey in winter. 53 cm.

Legs are yellow in summer

Great Black-backed Gull ▶

Britain's largest Gull. Not very common inland. Nests on rocky coasts. Often solitary. Legs pinkish. 66 cm.

◀ Common Gull

Some nest in Scotland and Ireland. Seen further south and often inland in winter. 41 cm.

Gull, Terns

Summer

◀ Herring Gull
Common on the coast in ports and seaside towns. Scrounges food from people and even nests on buildings. Young's plumage is mottled brown for first three years. 56 cm.

Arctic Tern in summer

Common Tern's bill has black tip

Arctic Tern ▶
Common Tern ▶
Both species most likely to be seen near sea, but Common Tern also nests inland. Both dive into sea to catch fish. 34 cm.

Summer

Summer

Winter

◀ Black Tern
A spring and autumn visitor to Britain. Can be seen flying low over lakes, dipping down to pick food from the surface. 24 cm.

Little Tern ▶
A summer visitor to Britain which nests in small groups on shingle beaches. Dives for fish. 24 cm.

Look for yellow bill with black tip

Summer

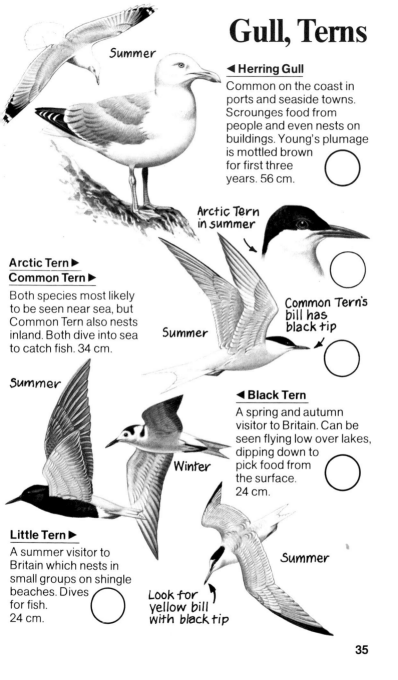

Owls

Barn Owl ▶

Its call is an eerie shriek.
Often nests in old
buildings or hollow
trees. Hunts small
mammals and
roosting birds.
34 cm.

Birds with dark
faces and
breasts are
found in north
and east Europe

◀ Little Owl

Small, flat-headed owl
Flies low over farmland
and hunts at dusk. Nes
in tree-holes. Bobs up
and down
when curious.
22 cm.

Bouncing
flight

Tawny Owl ▶

Calls with familiar "hoot".
Hunts at night where there
are woods or old trees.
Eats small
mammals or birds.
38 cm.

◀ Pygmy Owl

Smallest European owl.
Found in mountain forests,
but not in Britain. Has a
whistling "keeoo" call.
Hunts small birds
in flight.
16 cm.

Owls

Short-eared Owl ▶
Hunts in daylight and at dusk. Likes open country where it catches voles and other small mammals. Perches on the ground. Fierce-looking. 37 cm.

◀ Long-eared Owl
A secretive night-hunting owl of dense conifer woods. Roosts during the day. Long "ear" tufts cannot be seen in flight. 34 cm.

Tengmalm's Owl ▶
Small owl that lives in forests in northern and central Europe. Very rare visitor to Britain. Hunts at night. Nests in tree-holes. 25 cm.

◀ Scops Owl
Rare visitor to Britain from southern Europe. Gives its monotonous "kiu" call from a hidden perch. Hunts only at night. 19 cm.

Hoopoe, Nightjar, Cuckoo, Kingfisher

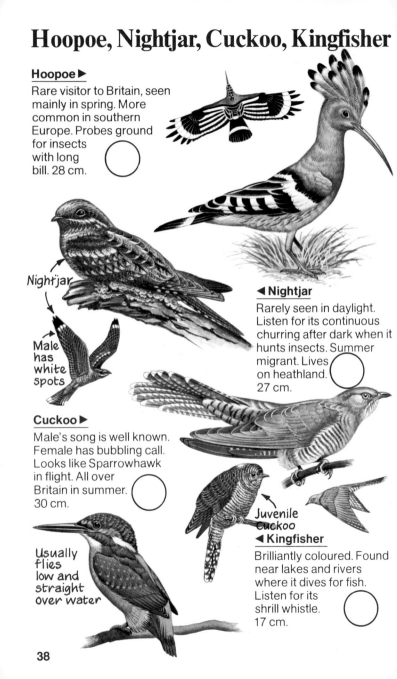

Hoopoe ▶

Rare visitor to Britain, seen mainly in spring. More common in southern Europe. Probes ground for insects with long bill. 28 cm.

Nightjar

Male has white spots

◀ Nightjar

Rarely seen in daylight. Listen for its continuous churring after dark when it hunts insects. Summer migrant. Lives on heathland. 27 cm.

Cuckoo ▶

Male's song is well known. Female has bubbling call. Looks like Sparrowhawk in flight. All over Britain in summer. 30 cm.

Juvenile Cuckoo

Usually flies low and straight over water

◀ Kingfisher

Brilliantly coloured. Found near lakes and rivers where it dives for fish. Listen for its shrill whistle. 17 cm.

Woodpeckers

Male has red crown

Female has red patch on back of head

▼ Great Spotted Woodpecker

Size of a Song Thrush. In woods all over Britain. Drums on trees in spring. 23 cm.

Large white patches on wings

▲ Black Woodpecker

Size of a Rook. In forests in Europe, especially old pine woods. Not in Britain. Can be confused with Crow in flight. 46 cm.

▼ Green Woodpecker

Size of a Town Pigeon. Often feeds on ground. Open woods and parks. Quite common in England and Wales. Rare in Scotland. Laugh-like call. 32 cm.

Striped back

Yellow-green rump

▲ Lesser Spotted Woodpecker

Sparrow-sized. Lacks white wing patches of Great Spotted. Male has red crown. Found in open woods. Not in Scotland. 14 cm.

Woodpeckers do not live in Ireland. They all have bouncing flight

Swift, Swallow, Martins

Swift ▶
A common migrant that visits Britain from May to August. Flies fast over towns and country in flocks. Listen for its screaming call. 17 cm.

Swift's tail is forked

Swallow's tail has streamers when adult

White underparts

◀ Swallow
Summer migrant seen from April to October. Prefers country, usually near water. Nests on rafters or ledges in buildings. 19 cm.

House Martin ▶
Summer migrant to Britain. Builds a cup-shaped nest under eaves. Is found in town and country. Like the Swallow, it catches insects in flight. 13 cm.

White rump

White underparts

Brown back

Brown band on breast

◀ Sand Martin
Summer migrant. Groups nest in holes in sandy cliffs and other soft banks. Often seen in flocks, catching insects over water. 12 cm.

Larks, Pipits, Dunnock

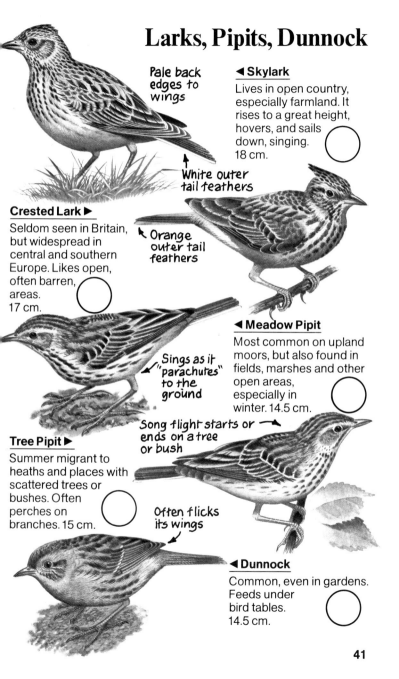

Pale back edges to wings

◄ **Skylark**
Lives in open country, especially farmland. It rises to a great height, hovers, and sails down, singing. 18 cm.

White outer tail feathers

Crested Lark ►
Seldom seen in Britain, but widespread in central and southern Europe. Likes open, often barren, areas. 17 cm.

Orange outer tail feathers

◄ **Meadow Pipit**
Most common on upland moors, but also found in fields, marshes and other open areas, especially in winter. 14.5 cm.

Sings as it "parachutes" to the ground

Song flight starts or ends on a tree or bush

Tree Pipit ►
Summer migrant to heaths and places with scattered trees or bushes. Often perches on branches. 15 cm.

Often flicks its wings

◄ **Dunnock**
Common, even in gardens. Feeds under bird tables. 14.5 cm.

Wagtails

Pied Wagtail ▶
White Wagtail ▶

White Wagtail is widespread in Europe, but in Britain we usually only see the Pied. Common, even in towns. 18 cm.

All the birds on this page wag their tails up and down.

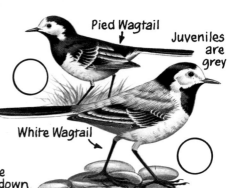

Pied Wagtail

Juveniles are grey

White Wagtail

◀ Grey Wagtail

Usually nests near fast-flowing water in hilly areas. Paler yellow in winter, when it visits lowland waters. Male has black throat. 18 cm.

♂

Summer

Blue-headed Wagtail Central Europe

♂

♂

Yellow Wagtail Britain and Ireland

Ashy-headed Wagtail Southern Europe

Yellow Wagtail ▶
Blue-headed Wagtail ▲

Summer visitor which likes grassy places near water. In Britain we usually see only the Yellow Wagtail. 17 cm.

♂

Spanish Wagtail Spain and Portugal

Females are duller coloured

Waxwing, Dipper, Wren, Shrikes

Resembles a Starling in flight

◀ **Waxwing**
Rare winter visitor from northern Europe. Feeds on berries and will visit gardens. 17 cm.

Dipper ▶
Likes fast-flowing rivers and streams in hilly areas. Bobs up and down on rocks in water. Submerges to find food. 18 cm.

Northern Europe

Britain and Central Europe

◀ **Wren**
Found almost everywhere. Loud song finishes with a a trill. Never keeps still for long. 9.5 cm.

Flies fast and straight on tiny, rounded wings

Red-backed Shrike ▶
Rare summer migrant to heaths in south-east England. Catches and eats insects, small birds, etc. 17 cm.

♂　♀

Stores food by sticking it on thorns

◀ **Great Grey Shrike**
Winter visitor to open country where it feeds on birds, mammals. etc. Flies low and often hovers. 24 cm.

43

Warblers

Sedge Warbler ▶
Summer migrant. Nests in thick vegetation, usually near water, but sometimes in drier areas. Sings from cover and is often difficult to see. 13 cm.

White stripe over eye

Rump is reddish-brown

◀ Reed Warbler
Summer visitor. Nests in reed beds or among waterside plants, mainly in the south of England. Hard to spot. Look for it flitting over reeds. 13 cm.

Garden Warbler ▶
Summer visitor. Sings from dense cover, and is hard to see. Likes woods with undergrowth or thick hedges. Song can be confused with Blackcap's. 14 cm.

Brown above, paler below

♂

Female's cap is reddish-brown

♀

◀ Blackcap
Common summer visitor to woods or places with trees. Always moving from perch to perch as it sings. 14 cm.

Warblers

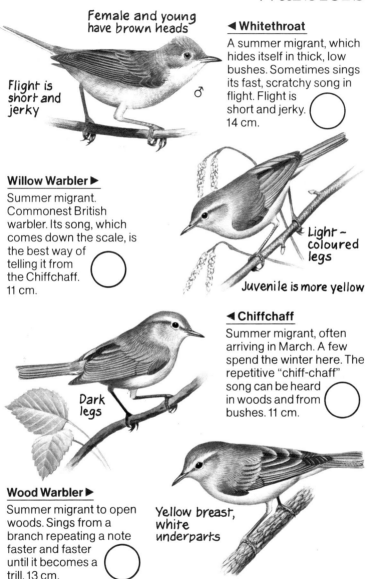

Female and young have brown heads

Flight is short and jerky

♂

◄ Whitethroat
A summer migrant, which hides itself in thick, low bushes. Sometimes sings its fast, scratchy song in flight. Flight is short and jerky. 14 cm.

Willow Warbler ►
Summer migrant. Commonest British warbler. Its song, which comes down the scale, is the best way of telling it from the Chiffchaff. 11 cm.

Light-coloured legs

Juvenile is more yellow

◄ Chiffchaff
Summer migrant, often arriving in March. A few spend the winter here. The repetitive "chiff-chaff" song can be heard in woods and from bushes. 11 cm.

Dark legs

Wood Warbler ►
Summer migrant to open woods. Sings from a branch repeating a note faster and faster until it becomes a trill. 13 cm.

Yellow breast, white underparts

Flycatchers, Chats

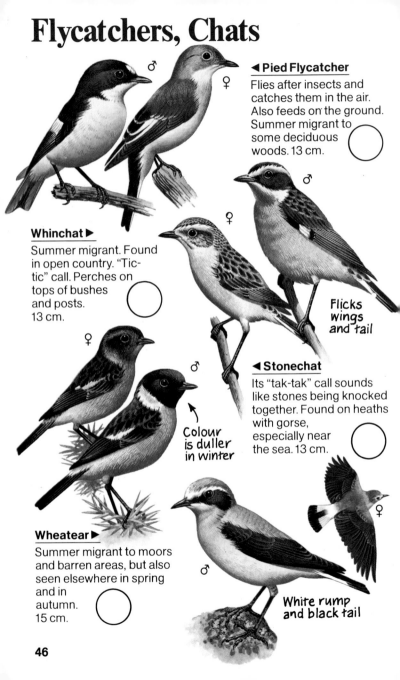

◄ Pied Flycatcher
Flies after insects and catches them in the air. Also feeds on the ground. Summer migrant to some deciduous woods. 13 cm.

Whinchat ►
Summer migrant. Found in open country. "Tic-tic" call. Perches on tops of bushes and posts. 13 cm.

Flicks wings and tail

◄ Stonechat
Its "tak-tak" call sounds like stones being knocked together. Found on heaths with gorse, especially near the sea. 13 cm.

Colour is duller in winter

Wheatear ►
Summer migrant to moors and barren areas, but also seen elsewhere in spring and in autumn. 15 cm.

White rump and black tail

Flycatchers, Chats

Spotted Flycatcher ▶
Summer migrant. Catches
insects in flight. Likes
open woods, parks
and gardens.
14 cm.

♀

Sits upright,
often on a
bare branch

◀ Redstart
Summer migrant to open
woods, parks and heaths.
Constantly
flickers its
tail. 14 cm.

♀

♂

♂

Black Redstart ▶
A few nest on buildings or on
cliffs in Britain. Some winter in
the south of England.
Flickers its tail.
14 cm.

◀ Robin
A woodland bird that is familiar in
gardens. It sings during winter
and spring. "Tic-tic" is its call of
alarm. Male and
female look alike.
14 cm.

Nightingale ▶
Secretive summer migrant.
Best found by listening
for its song
during May and
June. 17 cm.

Reddish tail

Thrushes, Oriole

Fieldfare ▶

Winter visitor, but a few nest in England and Scotland. Flocks can be seen in autumn, eating berries in hedgerows. 25.5 cm.

◀ Ring Ouzel

Summer migrant to moors and mountains. Visits lower regions on migration. Shyer than Blackbird. Listen for loud piping call. 24 cm.

♀

♂

Young are lighter and spottier than female

♀

♂

Blackbird ▶

Lives where there are trees and bushes, often in parks and gardens. Some Blackbirds are part albino and have some white feathers. 25 cm.

◀ Golden Oriole

Rare summer migrant most likely to be seen in thick woods of England or Wales. Difficult to see as it spends a lot of time in tree-tops. 24 cm.

♂

♀

48

Thrushes, Starling

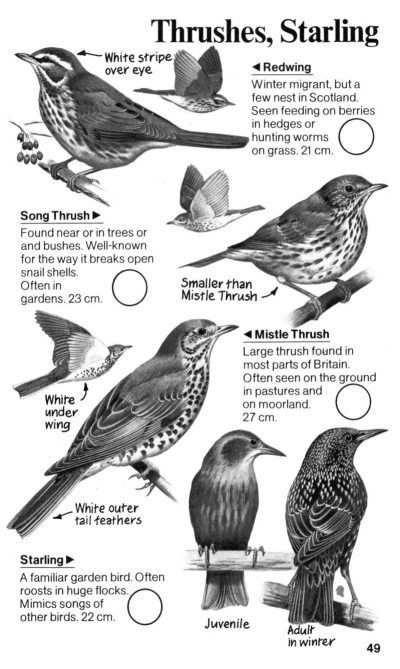

White stripe over eye

◄ Redwing
Winter migrant, but a few nest in Scotland. Seen feeding on berries in hedges or hunting worms on grass. 21 cm.

Song Thrush ►
Found near or in trees or and bushes. Well-known for the way it breaks open snail shells. Often in gardens. 23 cm.

Smaller than Mistle Thrush ➜

White under wing

◄ Mistle Thrush
Large thrush found in most parts of Britain. Often seen on the ground in pastures and on moorland. 27 cm.

◄ White outer tail feathers

Starling ►
A familiar garden bird. Often roosts in huge flocks. Mimics songs of other birds. 22 cm.

Juvenile

Adult in winter

49

Tits

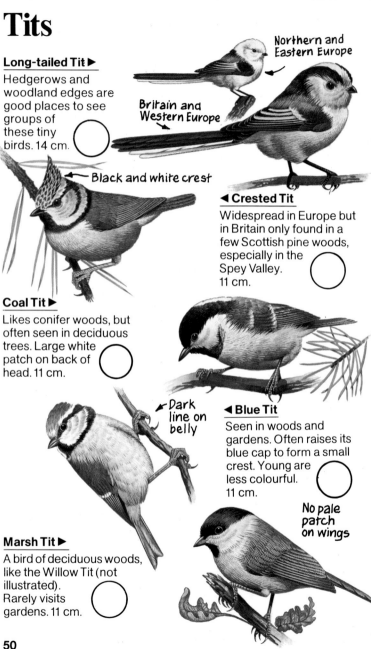

Long-tailed Tit ▶
Hedgerows and woodland edges are good places to see groups of these tiny birds. 14 cm.

Northern and Eastern Europe

Britain and Western Europe

Black and white crest

◀ Crested Tit
Widespread in Europe but in Britain only found in a few Scottish pine woods, especially in the Spey Valley. 11 cm.

Coal Tit ▶
Likes conifer woods, but often seen in deciduous trees. Large white patch on back of head. 11 cm.

Dark line on belly

◀ Blue Tit
Seen in woods and gardens. Often raises its blue cap to form a small crest. Young are less colourful. 11 cm.

No pale patch on wings

Marsh Tit ▶
A bird of deciduous woods, like the Willow Tit (not illustrated). Rarely visits gardens. 11 cm.

Tit, Nuthatch, Treecreeper, Crests

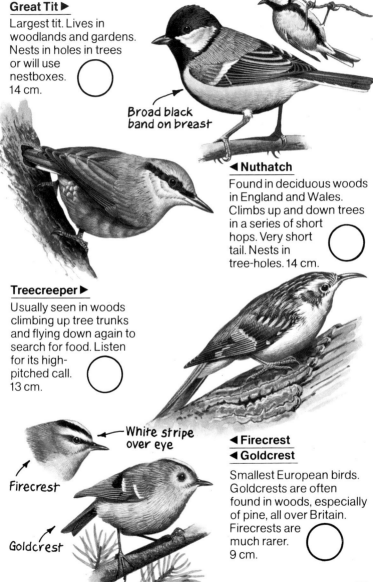

Great Tit ▶

Largest tit. Lives in woodlands and gardens. Nests in holes in trees or will use nestboxes. 14 cm.

Broad black band on breast

◀ Nuthatch

Found in deciduous woods in England and Wales. Climbs up and down trees in a series of short hops. Very short tail. Nests in tree-holes. 14 cm.

Treecreeper ▶

Usually seen in woods climbing up tree trunks and flying down again to search for food. Listen for its high-pitched call. 13 cm.

White stripe over eye

Firecrest

Goldcrest

◀ Firecrest
◀ Goldcrest

Smallest European birds. Goldcrests are often found in woods, especially of pine, all over Britain. Firecrests are much rarer. 9 cm.

Finches

Chaffinch ▶
Likely to be found wherever there are trees and bushes, including gardens. Often flocks with other finches in winter.
15 cm.

♀

♂

Male's head is brown in winter ↘

♂

◀ Brambling
Winter migrant from northern Europe. Flocks feed on grain and seeds. Likes fruit from beech trees.
15 cm.

♀

♂

Greenfinch ▶
A frequent visitor to gardens, especially in winter. Likely to nest wherever there are trees and bushes. 15 cm.

♀

♂

◀ Siskin
A small finch. Nests in conifers. Visits gardens in winter to feed on peanuts.
11 cm.

Finches

◄ Bullfinch
Often found on edges of woods, and in hedges or gardens. Eats seeds, but is a pest in orchards where it strips buds from fruit trees. 15 cm.

♀

♂

← White rump shows in flight

♂

♀

Linnet ►
Lives on heathland and farmland, but also found in towns, where it may visit gardens. Feeds on the seeds of weeds. Flocks in winter. 13 cm.

Mealy Redpoll

← Lesser Redpoll

◄ Lesser Redpoll
◄ Mealy Redpoll
The Lesser Redpoll is common in birch woods and forestry plantations in Britain. The Mealy lives in northern Europe. 12 cm.

Goldfinch ►
Feeds on thistle seeds and other weed seeds in open places. Nests in trees. 12 cm.

Yellow wing bar

53

Crossbill, Crows

♀ ♂

← Sparrow-sized

◄ Crossbill
Nests in Scottish pine woods. Rare elsewhere. Eats seeds from pine cones. 16 cm.

Jay ►
Secretive woodland bird. Will visit gardens. Listen for its harsh screeching call. Look for white rump in flight. 32 cm.

Raven ►
This large crow lives in wild rocky areas or on rocky coasts. Look for its wedge-shaped tail and huge bill. Croaks. 64 cm.

Grey on head ➤

Jackdaw ►
Small member of the crow family. Found where there are old trees, old buildings or cliffs. Nests in colonies. Often seen with Rooks. 33 cm.

Crows

◀ Carrion Crow
◀ Hooded Crow

Carrion is seen alone or in pairs. Hooded Crows form flocks. Carrion is more widespread than Hooded . 47 cm.

Carrion Crow — England, Wales and southern Scotland

Hooded Crow — Northern Scotland and Ireland

Rook ▶

Nests in "rookeries" in tops of trees. Is usually seen in flocks and likes farmland. Young lack bare skin round beak. Voice is a harsh "kaw". 46 cm.

Baggy thigh feathers

◀ Magpie

Seen in both town and country. Eats many eggs and young birds in spring. Forms flocks in winter. 46 cm.

55

Sparrows, Buntings

House Sparrow ▶

Very familiar bird. Lives near houses and even in city centres, where it eats scraps, etc. Often seen in flocks.
15 cm.

♀

♂

Brown cap and smudge below eye →

Male and female look alike

◀ Tree Sparrow

Usually nests in holes in trees or cliffs. Less common than House Sparrows in towns, but sometimes flocks with them in winter. 14 cm.

Yellowhammer ▶

Common in open country, especially farmland. Feeds on the ground. Forms flocks in winter. Sings from the tops of bushes.
17 cm.

♂

♀

♀

◀ Reed Bunting

Most common near water, but some nest in dry areas with long grass. Sometimes visits bird-tables in winter.
15 cm.

♀

♂

Corn Bunting ▶

Quite common in cornfields. Sings from posts, bushes or overhead wires.
18 cm.

Chapter 2
WILD FLOWERS

Introduction to Chapter 2

This chapter of the book contains an identification guide to some of the wild flowers of Britain and Europe. Not all of the species shown are common in Britain; some are very rare or do not grow here at all, but are included because they are common in other European countries.

The flowers are arranged by colour and the description next to each illustration points out the flower's most important identifying features, including its habitat. The pictures in circles next to the main illustrations show close-ups of flowers or sometimes the fruits or seeds of the plant. The plants are not drawn to scale but their average height (measured from the ground) is given. The last line of the description indicates the months that the plant is in flower.

Identifying wild flowers

Apart from a plant's size and habitat, there are several other important details you should note. Look at the shape and the arrangement of the leaves, the number of petals and stamens, any fruit or seeds that are present and whether the whole plant or any part of it is hairy or smooth. A magnifying glass is useful for examining the plant closely and for looking at insects you may find on it.

Tips on photography

Photographs provide a good record of the flowers you have found and are helpful for identifying those that are not in this book. Try to photograph the whole plant so that the stem and leaves are visible and if possible, take close-ups of the flower.

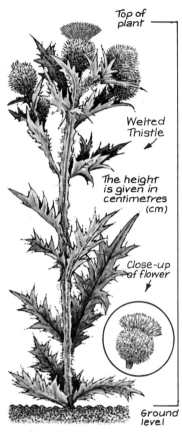

Top of plant

Welted Thistle

The height is given in centimetres (cm)

Close-up of flower

Ground level

If you lie flat on the ground and photograph from below, the plant or flower will be outlined against the sky and will stand out clearly. Sunlight filtering through the leaves shows up the veins in them. To prevent a flower from being lost among grass and leaves, prop a piece of black or coloured card behind it and photograph it against this background.

Parts of a plant

The following pages explain some of the terms that appear in this chapter and show some of the things you should look for when you are examining a plant.

Flowers

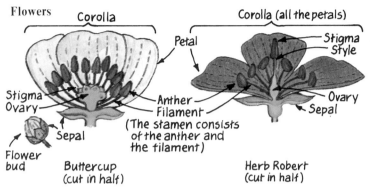

Buttercup (cut in half)

- Corolla
- Petal
- Stigma
- Ovary
- Sepal
- Anther
- Filament
- (The stamen consists of the anther and the filament)
- Flower bud

Herb Robert (cut in half)

- Corolla (all the petals)
- Stigma
- Style
- Ovary
- Sepal

The stigma, style and ovary make up the female reproductive organs and the stamens the male ones. Pollen grains from the stamens are received by the stigma and result in the growth of a seed inside the ovary

In most flowers the reproductive organs are surrounded by sepals and petals. Sepals, which are usually green, make up the outer part of the flower called the calyx. The petals make up the corolla. Petals may be arranged regularly or irregularly or they may be fused.

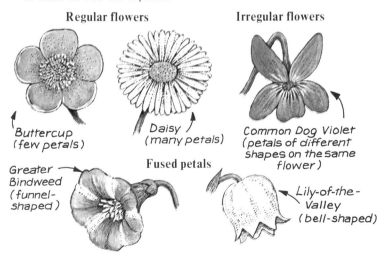

Regular flowers

Buttercup (few petals)

Daisy (many petals)

Irregular flowers

Common Dog Violet (petals of different shapes on the same flower)

Fused petals

Greater Bindweed (funnel-shaped)

Lily-of-the-Valley (bell-shaped)

Arrangement of flowers

On many plants the flowers are arranged in clusters or groups. Some of the more common forms are illustrated here.

Simple umbel: all the flower stalks grow from the same point at the top of the main stem.

Compound umbel: all the stalks grow from the same point and each has several flower stalks at the end.

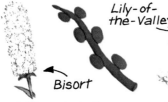

Spike: stalkless, single flowers on the main stem with the youngest flowers at the top of the stem.

Raceme: clusters are similar to a spike but the flowers are borne on stalks.

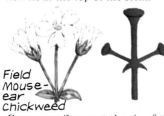

Cyme: one flower at the tip of the main stem with the younger ones on both sides beneath it.

One-sided cyme: one flower at the tip of the main stem with younger ones on one side beneath it.

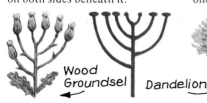

Corymb: flowers at the same level; stalks arise from different levels with the oldest on the outside.

Capitulum: flower head is made up of many densely packed, stalkless flowers.

Leaves

Most leaves consist of a stalk and a flattened blade. Below are seven different **simple leaves** of various shapes.

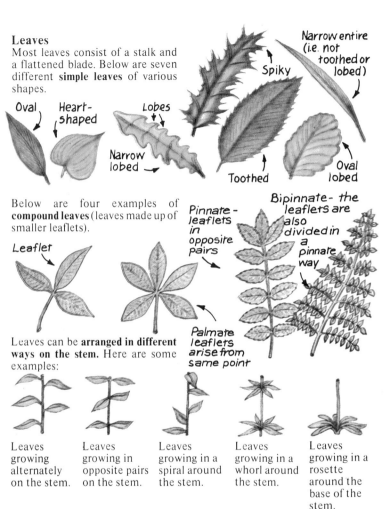

Oval

Heart-shaped

Lobes

Narrow lobed

Spiky

Narrow entire (i.e. not toothed or lobed)

Toothed

Oval lobed

Below are four examples of **compound leaves** (leaves made up of smaller leaflets).

Leaflet

Pinnate - leaflets in opposite pairs

Bipinnate- the leaflets are also divided in a pinnate way

Palmate leaflets arise from same point

Leaves can be **arranged in different ways on the stem.** Here are some examples:

Leaves growing alternately on the stem.

Leaves growing in opposite pairs on the stem.

Leaves growing in a spiral around the stem.

Leaves growing in a whorl around the stem.

Leaves growing in a rosette around the base of the stem.

Fruits and seeds

Fruits usually appear after the petals have withered and fallen. Most seeds are contained inside the fleshy or dry fruit.

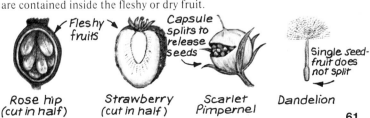

Fleshy fruits

Capsule splits to release seeds

Single seed-fruit does not split

Rose hip (cut in half)

Strawberry (cut in half)

Scarlet Pimpernel

Dandelion

61

Look for these flowers in damp places, such as ditches, marshes and water meadows.

Lesser Celandine ▶

A small, creeping plant with glossy, heart-shaped leaves. Shiny yellow flowers. Look in damp shady woods and waysides. 7 cm tall. March-May.

◀ Alternate-leaved Golden Saxifrage

Small plant with round, toothed leaves, and greenish yellow flowers. Look in wet places. 7 cm tall. April-July.

Each flower has four yellow sepals

Creeping Buttercup ▶

Look for the long runners near the ground. Hairy, deeply-divided leaves. Shiny yellow flowers. Common weed of grassy places. May-Aug.

Runner

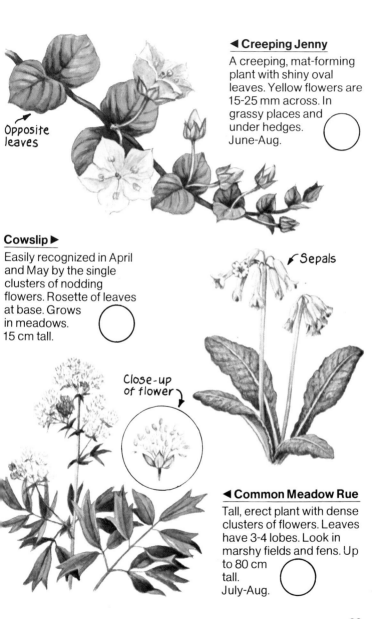

◄ Creeping Jenny

A creeping, mat-forming plant with shiny oval leaves. Yellow flowers are 15-25 mm across. In grassy places and under hedges.
June-Aug.

Opposite leaves

Cowslip ►

Easily recognized in April and May by the single clusters of nodding flowers. Rosette of leaves at base. Grows in meadows.
15 cm tall.

Sepals

Close-up of flower

◄ Common Meadow Rue

Tall, erect plant with dense clusters of flowers. Leaves have 3-4 lobes. Look in marshy fields and fens. Up to 80 cm tall.
July-Aug.

Look for these flowers, and those on page 11, in woods, hedgerows and heaths.

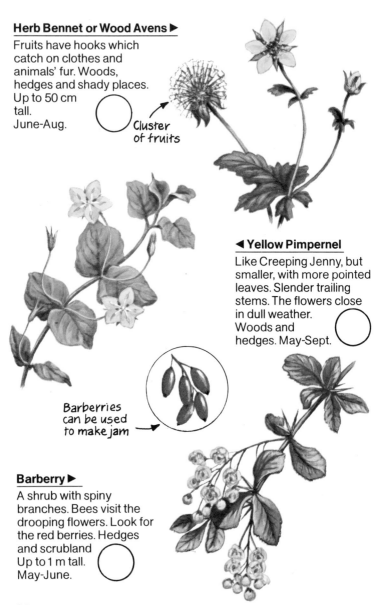

Herb Bennet or Wood Avens ▶

Fruits have hooks which catch on clothes and animals' fur. Woods, hedges and shady places. Up to 50 cm tall. June-Aug.

Cluster of fruits

◀ Yellow Pimpernel

Like Creeping Jenny, but smaller, with more pointed leaves. Slender trailing stems. The flowers close in dull weather. Woods and hedges. May-Sept.

Barberries can be used to make jam

Barberry ▶

A shrub with spiny branches. Bees visit the drooping flowers. Look for the red berries. Hedges and scrubland Up to 1 m tall. May-June.

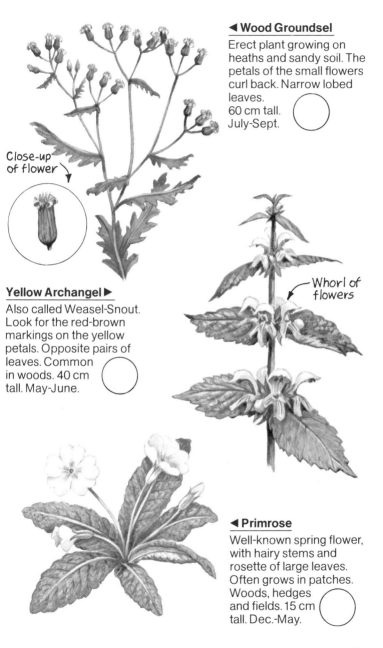

◄ Wood Groundsel
Erect plant growing on heaths and sandy soil. The petals of the small flowers curl back. Narrow lobed leaves.
60 cm tall.
July-Sept.

Close-up of flower ↘

Yellow Archangel ►
Also called Weasel-Snout. Look for the red-brown markings on the yellow petals. Opposite pairs of leaves. Common in woods. 40 cm tall. May-June.

Whorl of flowers

◄ Primrose
Well-known spring flower, with hairy stems and rosette of large leaves. Often grows in patches. Woods, hedges and fields. 15 cm tall. Dec.-May.

Look for these flowers, and those on page 13, in open grassy places, such as heaths and commons.

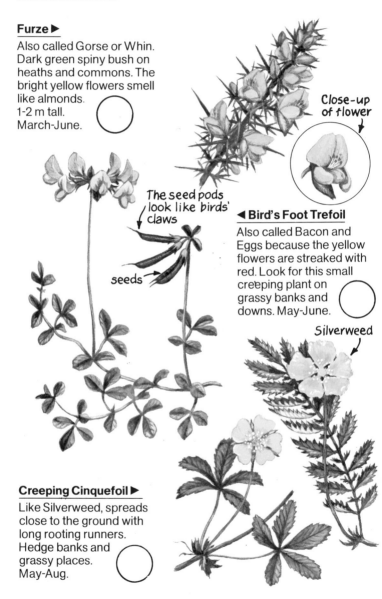

Furze ▶

Also called Gorse or Whin. Dark green spiny bush on heaths and commons. The bright yellow flowers smell like almonds.
1-2 m tall.
March-June.

Close-up of flower

The seed pods look like birds' claws

seeds

◀ Bird's Foot Trefoil

Also called Bacon and Eggs because the yellow flowers are streaked with red. Look for this small creeping plant on grassy banks and downs. May-June.

Silverweed

Creeping Cinquefoil ▶

Like Silverweed, spreads close to the ground with long rooting runners. Hedge banks and grassy places.
May-Aug.

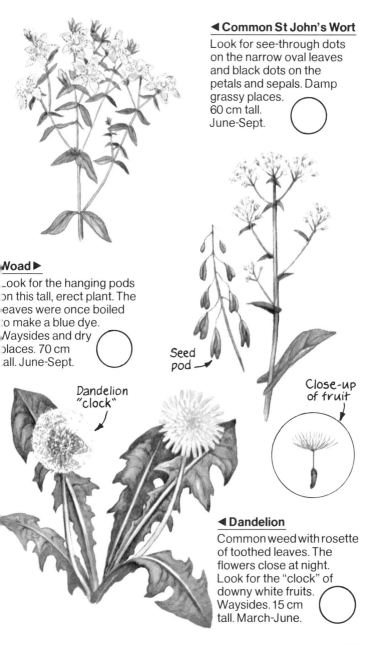

◄ Common St John's Wort

Look for see-through dots on the narrow oval leaves and black dots on the petals and sepals. Damp grassy places.
60 cm tall.
June-Sept.

Woad ►

Look for the hanging pods on this tall, erect plant. The leaves were once boiled to make a blue dye. Waysides and dry places. 70 cm tall. June-Sept.

Seed pod →

Dandelion "clock"

Close-up of fruit

◄ Dandelion

Common weed with rosette of toothed leaves. The flowers close at night. Look for the "clock" of downy white fruits. Waysides. 15 cm tall. March-June.

Stonecrop ▶

Also called Wallpepper.
Mat-forming plant with
star-shaped flowers. The
thick fleshy leaves have
a peppery taste.
Dunes, shingle and
walls. June-July.

Close-up
of a flower

Leaves

◀ Purslane

A low spreading plant with
red stems. The fleshy oval-
shaped leaves are in
opposite pairs. A weed of
fields and waste
places.
May-Oct.

Close-up
of a flower

Golden Rod ▶

Erect plant with flowers
in clusters. Leaves are
narrower and more pointed
near top of plant. Woods,
banks and cliffs.
40 cm tall.
July-Sept.

Leaves
broader
near bottom
of plant

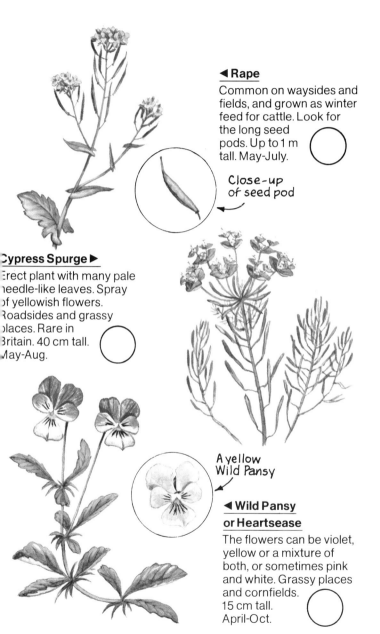

◄ Rape

Common on waysides and fields, and grown as winter feed for cattle. Look for the long seed pods. Up to 1 m tall. May-July.

Close-up of seed pod

Cypress Spurge ►

Erect plant with many pale needle-like leaves. Spray of yellowish flowers. Roadsides and grassy places. Rare in Britain. 40 cm tall. May-Aug.

A yellow Wild Pansy

◄ Wild Pansy or Heartsease

The flowers can be violet, yellow or a mixture of both, or sometimes pink and white. Grassy places and cornfields. 15 cm tall. April-Oct.

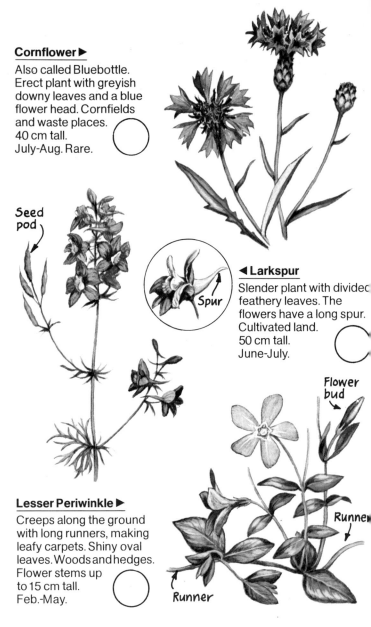

Cornflower ▶

Also called Bluebottle.
Erect plant with greyish
downy leaves and a blue
flower head. Cornfields
and waste places.
40 cm tall.
July-Aug. Rare.

Seed
pod

Spur

◀ Larkspur

Slender plant with divided
feathery leaves. The
flowers have a long spur.
Cultivated land.
50 cm tall.
June-July.

Flower
bud

Runner

Lesser Periwinkle ▶

Creeps along the ground
with long runners, making
leafy carpets. Shiny oval
leaves. Woods and hedges.
Flower stems up
to 15 cm tall.
Feb.-May.

Runner

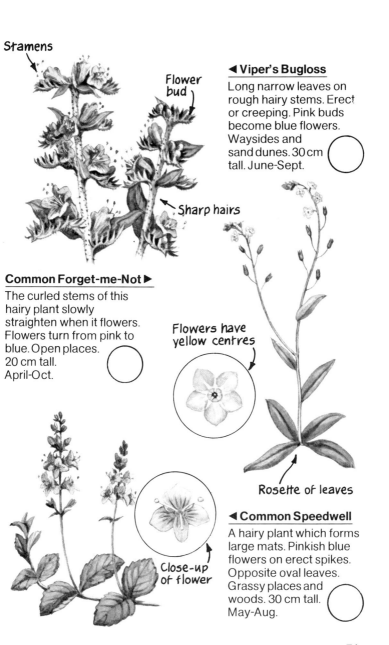

Stamens

Flower bud

Sharp hairs

◀ Viper's Bugloss
Long narrow leaves on rough hairy stems. Erect or creeping. Pink buds become blue flowers. Waysides and sand dunes. 30 cm tall. June-Sept.

Common Forget-me-Not ▶
The curled stems of this hairy plant slowly straighten when it flowers. Flowers turn from pink to blue. Open places. 20 cm tall. April-Oct.

Flowers have yellow centres

Rosette of leaves

Close-up of flower

◀ Common Speedwell
A hairy plant which forms large mats. Pinkish blue flowers on erect spikes. Opposite oval leaves. Grassy places and woods. 30 cm tall. May-Aug.

71

Look for the flowers shown on this page in damp places.

Common Monkshood ▶

Also called Wolfsbane.
Notice hood on flowers
and the deeply-divided
leaves. Near streams and
in damp woods.
70 cm tall.
June-Sept.

Flower is
shaped like a
monk's hood

◀ Brooklime

Creeping plant with erect
reddish stems. Shiny oval
leaves in opposite pairs.
Used to be eaten in
salads. Wet
places. 30 cm tall.
May-Sept.

Bugle ▶

Creeping plant with erect
flower spikes. Purplish
stem is hairy on two
sides. Forms carpets in
damp woods.
10-20 cm tall.
May-June.

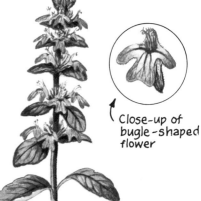

Close-up of
bugle-shaped
flower

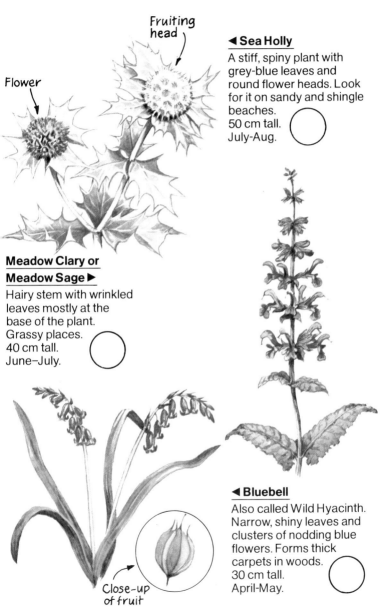

Fruiting
head

Flower

◀ Sea Holly
A stiff, spiny plant with
grey-blue leaves and
round flower heads. Look
for it on sandy and shingle
beaches.
50 cm tall.
July-Aug.

Meadow Clary or
Meadow Sage ▶
Hairy stem with wrinkled
leaves mostly at the
base of the plant.
Grassy places.
40 cm tall.
June–July.

◀ Bluebell
Also called Wild Hyacinth.
Narrow, shiny leaves and
clusters of nodding blue
flowers. Forms thick
carpets in woods.
30 cm tall.
April-May.

Close-up
of fruit

Look for the flowers shown on this page in woods or hedges.

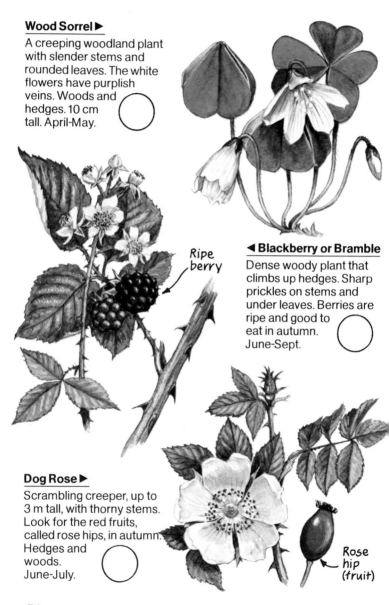

Wood Sorrel ▶
A creeping woodland plant with slender stems and rounded leaves. The white flowers have purplish veins. Woods and hedges. 10 cm tall. April-May.

Ripe berry

◀ Blackberry or Bramble
Dense woody plant that climbs up hedges. Sharp prickles on stems and under leaves. Berries are ripe and good to eat in autumn. June-Sept.

Dog Rose ▶
Scrambling creeper, up to 3 m tall, with thorny stems. Look for the red fruits, called rose hips, in autumn. Hedges and woods. June-July.

Rose hip (fruit)

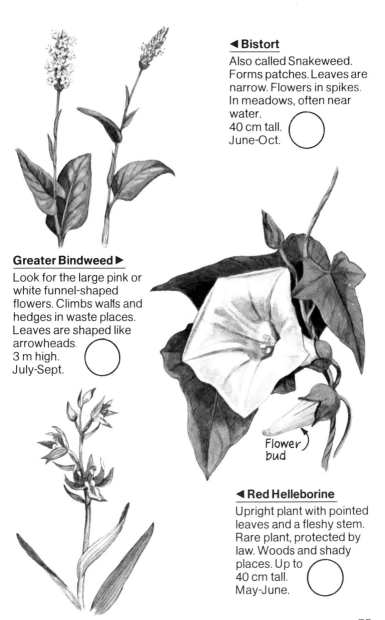

◀ Bistort

Also called Snakeweed.
Forms patches. Leaves are
narrow. Flowers in spikes.
In meadows, often near
water.
40 cm tall.
June-Oct.

Greater Bindweed ▶

Look for the large pink or
white funnel-shaped
flowers. Climbs walls and
hedges in waste places.
Leaves are shaped like
arrowheads.
3 m high.
July-Sept.

Flower
bud

◀ Red Helleborine

Upright plant with pointed
leaves and a fleshy stem.
Rare plant, protected by
law. Woods and shady
places. Up to
40 cm tall.
May-June.

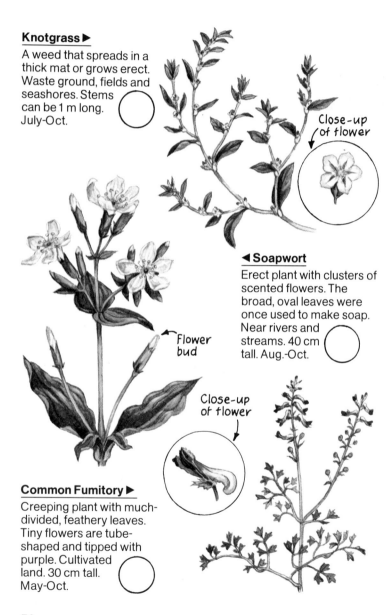

Knotgrass ▶

A weed that spreads in a
thick mat or grows erect.
Waste ground, fields and
seashores. Stems
can be 1 m long.
July-Oct.

Close-up
of flower

◀ Soapwort

Erect plant with clusters of
scented flowers. The
broad, oval leaves were
once used to make soap.
Near rivers and
streams. 40 cm
tall. Aug.-Oct.

Flower
bud

Close-up
of flower

Common Fumitory ▶

Creeping plant with much-
divided, feathery leaves.
Tiny flowers are tube-
shaped and tipped with
purple. Cultivated
land. 30 cm tall.
May-Oct.

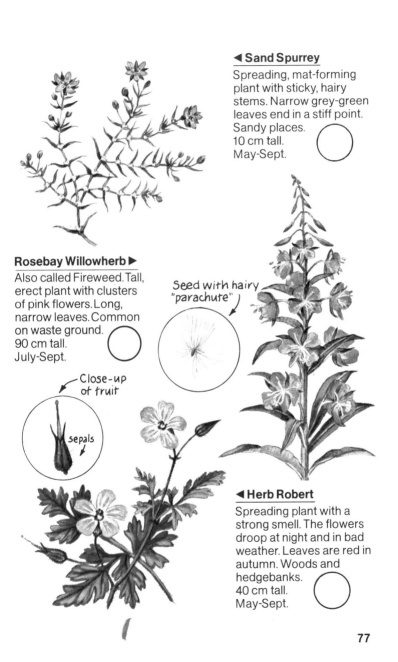

◀ Sand Spurrey

Spreading, mat-forming
plant with sticky, hairy
stems. Narrow grey-green
leaves end in a stiff point.
Sandy places.
10 cm tall.
May-Sept.

Rosebay Willowherb ▶

Also called Fireweed. Tall,
erect plant with clusters
of pink flowers. Long,
narrow leaves. Common
on waste ground.
90 cm tall.
July-Sept.

Seed with hairy
"parachute"

Close-up
of fruit

sepals

◀ Herb Robert

Spreading plant with a
strong smell. The flowers
droop at night and in bad
weather. Leaves are red in
autumn. Woods and
hedgebanks.
40 cm tall.
May-Sept.

Look for these flowers on heaths and moors.

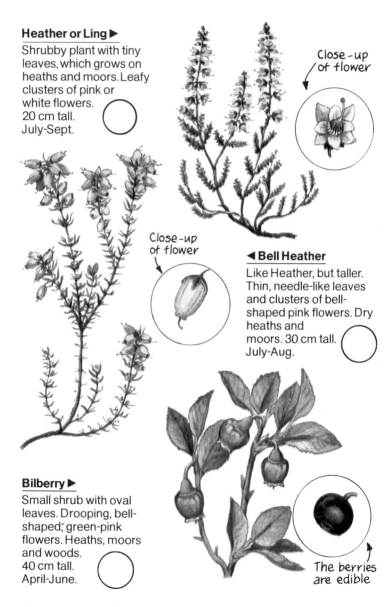

Heather or Ling ▶
Shrubby plant with tiny leaves, which grows on heaths and moors. Leafy clusters of pink or white flowers. 20 cm tall. July-Sept.

Close-up of flower

Close-up of flower

◀ Bell Heather
Like Heather, but taller. Thin, needle-like leaves and clusters of bell-shaped pink flowers. Dry heaths and moors. 30 cm tall. July-Aug.

Bilberry ▶
Small shrub with oval leaves. Drooping, bell-shaped, green-pink flowers. Heaths, moors and woods. 40 cm tall. April-June.

The berries are edible

Look for these flowers in dry, grassy places.

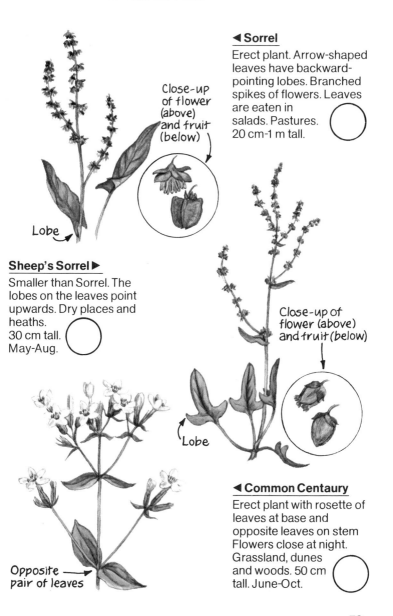

◀ Sorrel

Erect plant. Arrow-shaped leaves have backward-pointing lobes. Branched spikes of flowers. Leaves are eaten in salads. Pastures. 20 cm-1 m tall.

Close-up of flower (above) and fruit (below)

Lobe

Sheep's Sorrel ▶

Smaller than Sorrel. The lobes on the leaves point upwards. Dry places and heaths. 30 cm tall. May-Aug.

Close-up of flower (above) and fruit (below)

Lobe

◀ Common Centaury

Erect plant with rosette of leaves at base and opposite leaves on stem Flowers close at night. Grassland, dunes and woods. 50 cm tall. June-Oct.

Opposite pair of leaves

Ragged Robin ▶

Flowers have ragged pink petals. Erect plant with a forked stem and narrow, pointed leaves. Damp meadows, marshes and woods.
30-70 cm tall.
May-June.

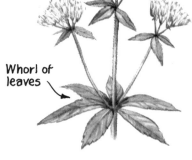

A bract is a kind of small leaf near the flower

Grooved stem

◀ Knapweed or Hard-head

Erect plant with brush-like pink flowers growing from black bracts. Grassland and waysides.
40 cm tall.
June-Sept.

Hemp Agrimony ▶

Tough, erect plant with downy stem. Grows in patches in damp places. Attracts butterflies.
Up to 120 cm tall.
July–Sept.

Whorl of leaves

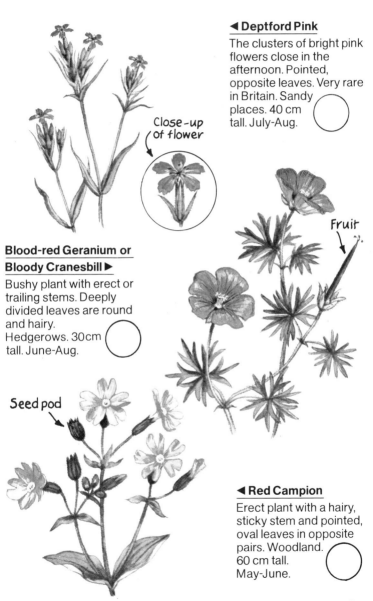

◄ Deptford Pink

The clusters of bright pink flowers close in the afternoon. Pointed, opposite leaves. Very rare in Britain. Sandy places. 40 cm tall. July-Aug.

Close-up of flower

Fruit

Blood-red Geranium or
Bloody Cranesbill ►

Bushy plant with erect or trailing stems. Deeply divided leaves are round and hairy. Hedgerows. 30cm tall. June-Aug.

Seed pod

◄ Red Campion

Erect plant with a hairy, sticky stem and pointed, oval leaves in opposite pairs. Woodland. 60 cm tall. May-June.

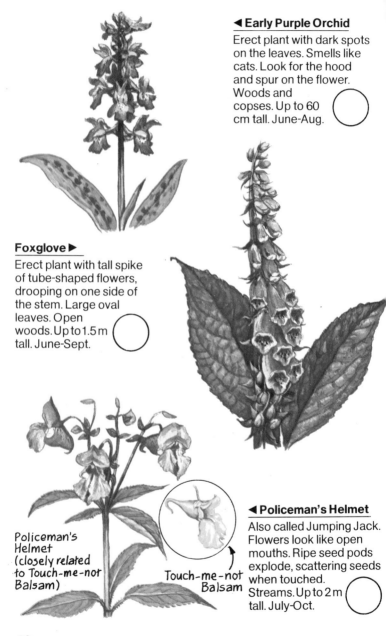

◄ Early Purple Orchid

Erect plant with dark spots
on the leaves. Smells like
cats. Look for the hood
and spur on the flower.
Woods and
copses. Up to 60
cm tall. June-Aug.

Foxglove ►

Erect plant with tall spike
of tube-shaped flowers,
drooping on one side of
the stem. Large oval
leaves. Open
woods. Up to 1.5 m
tall. June-Sept.

Policeman's
Helmet
(closely related
to Touch-me-not
Balsam)

Touch-me-not
Balsam

◄ Policeman's Helmet

Also called Jumping Jack.
Flowers look like open
mouths. Ripe seed pods
explode, scattering seeds
when touched.
Streams. Up to 2 m
tall. July-Oct.

Look for the flowers shown on this page in woods or hedgerows.

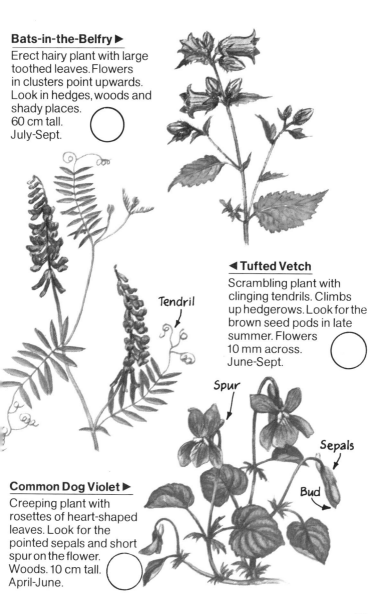

Bats-in-the-Belfry ▶
Erect hairy plant with large toothed leaves. Flowers in clusters point upwards. Look in hedges, woods and shady places.
60 cm tall.
July-Sept.

Tendril

◀ Tufted Vetch
Scrambling plant with clinging tendrils. Climbs up hedgerows. Look for the brown seed pods in late summer. Flowers 10 mm across.
June-Sept.

Spur

Sepals

Bud

Common Dog Violet ▶
Creeping plant with rosettes of heart-shaped leaves. Look for the pointed sepals and short spur on the flower.
Woods. 10 cm tall.
April-June.

Look in fields and other grassy places for these flowers.

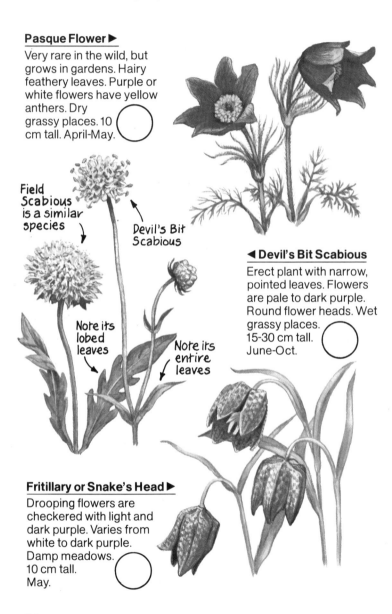

Pasque Flower ▶
Very rare in the wild, but grows in gardens. Hairy feathery leaves. Purple or white flowers have yellow anthers. Dry grassy places. 10 cm tall. April-May.

Field Scabious is a similar species

Devil's Bit Scabious

Note its lobed leaves

Note its entire leaves

◀ Devil's Bit Scabious
Erect plant with narrow, pointed leaves. Flowers are pale to dark purple. Round flower heads. Wet grassy places. 15-30 cm tall. June-Oct.

Fritillary or Snake's Head ▶
Drooping flowers are checkered with light and dark purple. Varies from white to dark purple. Damp meadows. 10 cm tall. May.

You may see these flowers on old walls.

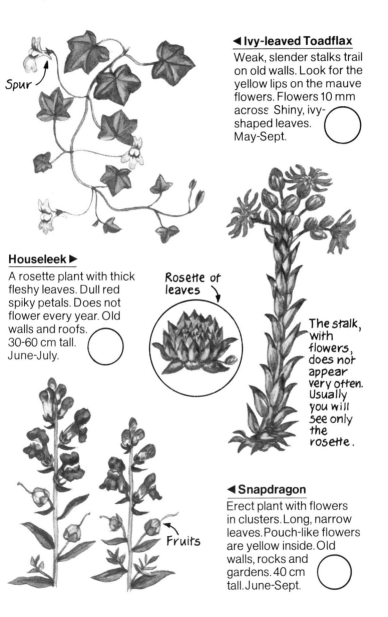

Spur

◄ Ivy-leaved Toadflax
Weak, slender stalks trail on old walls. Look for the yellow lips on the mauve flowers. Flowers 10 mm across. Shiny, ivy-shaped leaves. May-Sept.

Houseleek ►
A rosette plant with thick fleshy leaves. Dull red spiky petals. Does not flower every year. Old walls and roofs. 30-60 cm tall. June-July.

Rosette of leaves

The stalk, with flowers, does not appear very often. Usually you will see only the rosette.

Fruits

◄ Snapdragon
Erect plant with flowers in clusters. Long, narrow leaves. Pouch-like flowers are yellow inside. Old walls, rocks and gardens. 40 cm tall. June-Sept.

Look for these flowers in cornfields and on farmland.

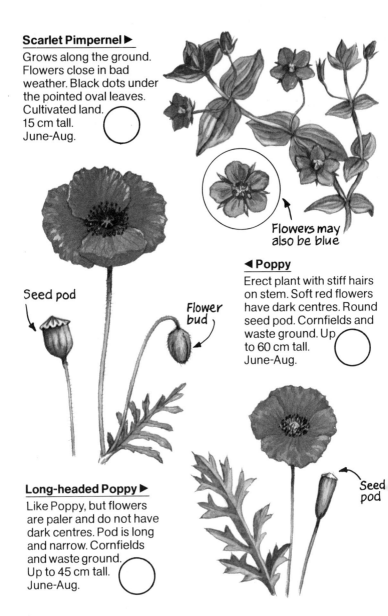

Scarlet Pimpernel ▶

Grows along the ground. Flowers close in bad weather. Black dots under the pointed oval leaves. Cultivated land. 15 cm tall. June-Aug.

Flowers may also be blue

Seed pod

Flower bud

◀ Poppy

Erect plant with stiff hairs on stem. Soft red flowers have dark centres. Round seed pod. Cornfields and waste ground. Up to 60 cm tall. June-Aug.

Seed pod

Long-headed Poppy ▶

Like Poppy, but flowers are paler and do not have dark centres. Pod is long and narrow. Cornfields and waste ground. Up to 45 cm tall. June-Aug.

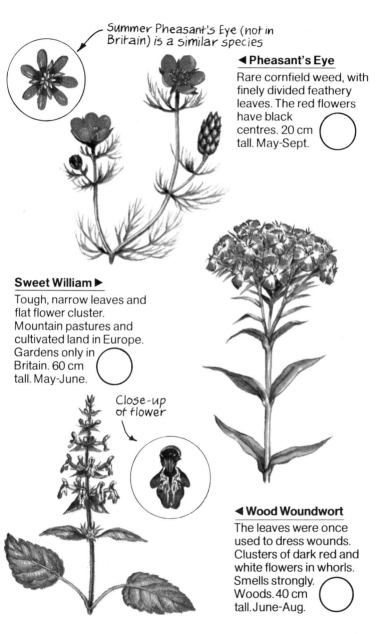

Summer Pheasant's Eye (not in Britain) is a similar species

◄ Pheasant's Eye

Rare cornfield weed, with finely divided feathery leaves. The red flowers have black centres. 20 cm tall. May-Sept.

Sweet William ►

Tough, narrow leaves and flat flower cluster. Mountain pastures and cultivated land in Europe. Gardens only in Britain. 60 cm tall. May-June.

Close-up of flower

◄ Wood Woundwort

The leaves were once used to dress wounds. Clusters of dark red and white flowers in whorls. Smells strongly. Woods. 40 cm tall. June-Aug.

87

The flowers on these two pages can be found in woodlands, quite early in the year.

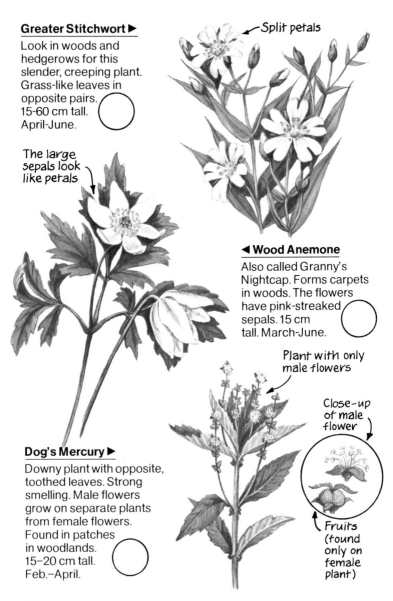

Greater Stitchwort ▶

Look in woods and hedgerows for this slender, creeping plant. Grass-like leaves in opposite pairs. 15-60 cm tall. April-June.

Split petals

The large sepals look like petals

◀ Wood Anemone

Also called Granny's Nightcap. Forms carpets in woods. The flowers have pink-streaked sepals. 15 cm tall. March-June.

Plant with only male flowers

Close-up of male flower

Dog's Mercury ▶

Downy plant with opposite, toothed leaves. Strong smelling. Male flowers grow on separate plants from female flowers. Found in patches in woodlands. 15–20 cm tall. Feb.–April.

Fruits (found only on female plant)

◄ Ramsons or Wood Garlic

Smells of garlic. Broad,
bright green leaves grow
from a bulb. Forms carpets
in damp woods, often with
Bluebells.
10-25 cm tall.
April-June.

Notice the
long veins
that run from
one end of
the leaf to
the other

Lily-of-the-Valley ►

Grows in dry woods.
Broad, dark green leaves
and sweet-smelling
flowers. Red berries in
summer. Also a
garden plant. 20
cm tall. May-June.

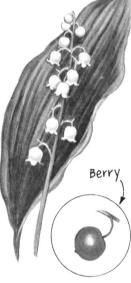

Berry

◄ Snowdrop

Welcomed as the first
flower of the new year.
Dark green, narrow leaves.
Nodding white flowers.
Woods.
20 cm tall.
Jan.-March.

Look for these flowers in hedges or woods.

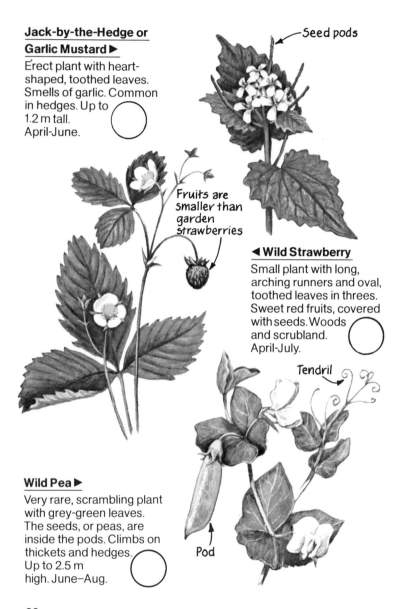

Jack-by-the-Hedge or Garlic Mustard ▶

Seed pods

Erect plant with heart-shaped, toothed leaves. Smells of garlic. Common in hedges. Up to 1.2 m tall. April-June.

Fruits are smaller than garden strawberries

◀ Wild Strawberry

Small plant with long, arching runners and oval, toothed leaves in threes. Sweet red fruits, covered with seeds. Woods and scrubland. April-July.

Tendril

Wild Pea ▶

Very rare, scrambling plant with grey-green leaves. The seeds, or peas, are inside the pods. Climbs on thickets and hedges. Up to 2.5 m high. June–Aug.

Pod

Look for these flowers in hedges and waysides.

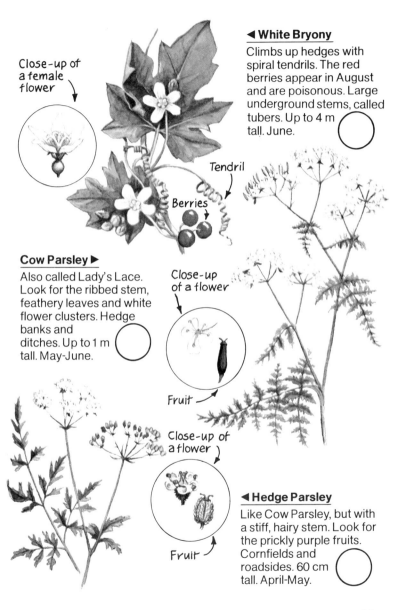

Close-up of a female flower

◀ White Bryony

Climbs up hedges with spiral tendrils. The red berries appear in August and are poisonous. Large underground stems, called tubers. Up to 4 m tall. June.

Tendril

Berries

Cow Parsley ▶

Also called Lady's Lace. Look for the ribbed stem, feathery leaves and white flower clusters. Hedge banks and ditches. Up to 1 m tall. May-June.

Close-up of a flower

Fruit

Close-up of a flower

◀ Hedge Parsley

Like Cow Parsley, but with a stiff, hairy stem. Look for the prickly purple fruits. Cornfields and roadsides. 60 cm tall. April-May.

Fruit

These flowers can be found in or near fresh water (streams, ponds, etc.).

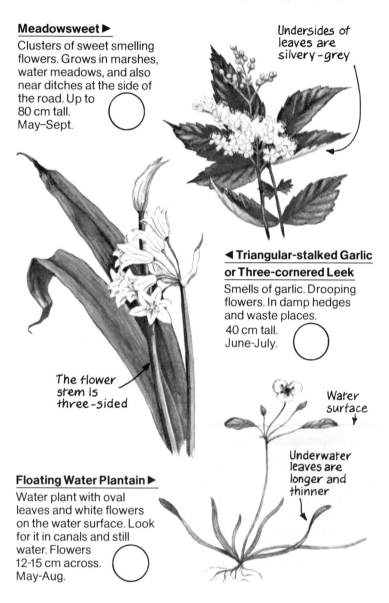

Meadowsweet ▶

Clusters of sweet smelling flowers. Grows in marshes, water meadows, and also near ditches at the side of the road. Up to 80 cm tall. May–Sept.

Undersides of leaves are silvery-grey

◀ Triangular-stalked Garlic or Three-cornered Leek

Smells of garlic. Drooping flowers. In damp hedges and waste places. 40 cm tall. June-July.

The flower stem is three-sided

Water surface

Underwater leaves are longer and thinner

Floating Water Plantain ▶

Water plant with oval leaves and white flowers on the water surface. Look for it in canals and still water. Flowers 12-15 cm across. May-Aug.

These flowers can be found in or near fresh water (streams, ponds, etc.).

◀ Water Crowfoot
Water plant whose roots are anchored in the mud at the bottom of ponds and streams. Flowers (10–20 mm across) cover the water surface. May–June.

These leaves are on the water surface

Fine, underwater leaves

Water Soldier ▶
Under water except when it flowers. Long saw-like leaves then show above the surface. Flowers 30-40 mm across. Ponds, canals, ditches. June-Aug.

Bud

◀ Frogbit
Rises to the surface in spring, and spreads with long runners. Shiny round leaves grow in tufts. Flowers 20 mm across. Canals and ponds. July-Aug.

Runner

Look for these flowers in fields and other grassy places.

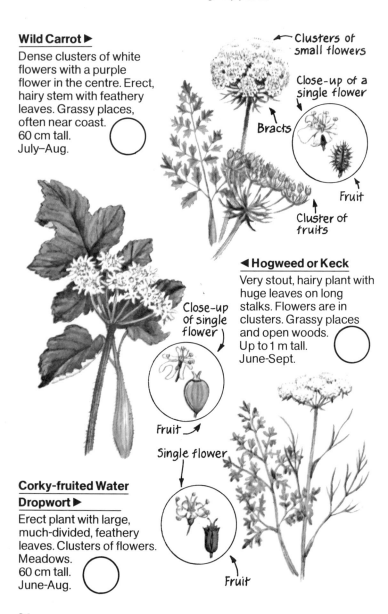

Wild Carrot ▶

Dense clusters of white flowers with a purple flower in the centre. Erect, hairy stem with feathery leaves. Grassy places, often near coast.
60 cm tall.
July–Aug.

Clusters of small flowers

Close-up of a single flower

Bracts

Fruit

Cluster of fruits

Close-up of single flower

Fruit

◀ Hogweed or Keck

Very stout, hairy plant with huge leaves on long stalks. Flowers are in clusters. Grassy places and open woods.
Up to 1 m tall.
June-Sept.

Single flower

Corky-fruited Water Dropwort ▶

Erect plant with large, much-divided, feathery leaves. Clusters of flowers. Meadows.
60 cm tall.
June-Aug.

Fruit

Look for these flowers in fields and other grassy places.

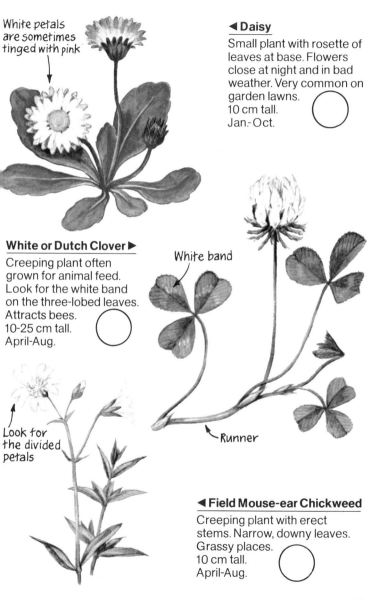

White petals are sometimes tinged with pink

◄ Daisy
Small plant with rosette of leaves at base. Flowers close at night and in bad weather. Very common on garden lawns.
10 cm tall.
Jan.-Oct.

White or Dutch Clover ►
Creeping plant often grown for animal feed. Look for the white band on the three-lobed leaves. Attracts bees.
10-25 cm tall.
April-Aug.

White band

Look for the divided petals

Runner

◄ Field Mouse-ear Chickweed
Creeping plant with erect stems. Narrow, downy leaves. Grassy places.
10 cm tall.
April-Aug.

Look for these flowers on cultivated land, waste land and waysides.

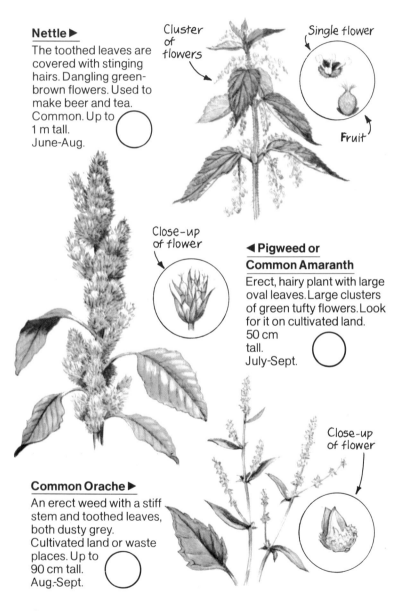

Nettle ▶

The toothed leaves are covered with stinging hairs. Dangling green-brown flowers. Used to make beer and tea. Common. Up to 1 m tall. June-Aug.

Cluster of flowers

Single flower

Fruit

Close-up of flower

◀ Pigweed or Common Amaranth

Erect, hairy plant with large oval leaves. Large clusters of green tufty flowers. Look for it on cultivated land. 50 cm tall. July-Sept.

Close-up of flower

Common Orache ▶

An erect weed with a stiff stem and toothed leaves, both dusty grey. Cultivated land or waste places. Up to 90 cm tall. Aug.-Sept.

Look for these flowers on cultivated land, waste land and waysides.

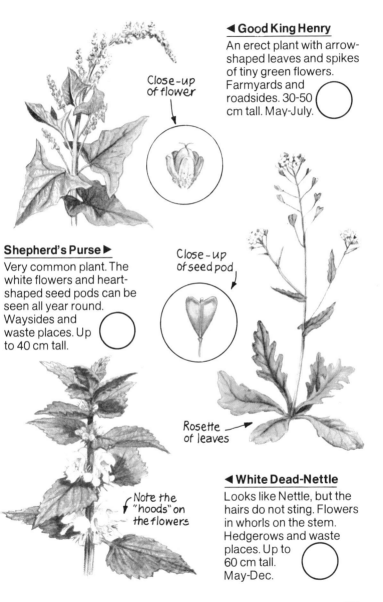

◀ Good King Henry
An erect plant with arrow-shaped leaves and spikes of tiny green flowers. Farmyards and roadsides. 30-50 cm tall. May-July.

Close-up of flower

Shepherd's Purse ▶
Very common plant. The white flowers and heart-shaped seed pods can be seen all year round. Waysides and waste places. Up to 40 cm tall.

Close-up of seed pod

Rosette of leaves

Note the "hoods" on the flowers

◀ White Dead-Nettle
Looks like Nettle, but the hairs do not sting. Flowers in whorls on the stem. Hedgerows and waste places. Up to 60 cm tall. May-Dec.

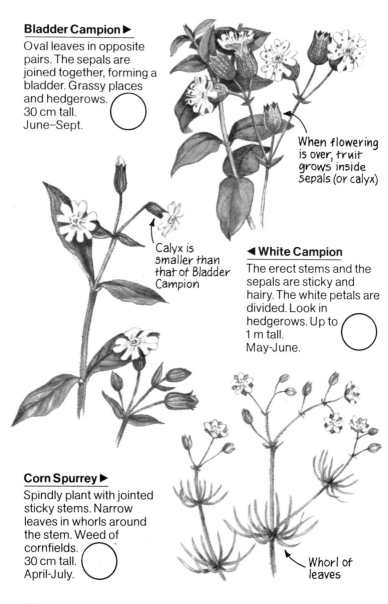

Bladder Campion ▶

Oval leaves in opposite pairs. The sepals are joined together, forming a bladder. Grassy places and hedgerows. 30 cm tall. June–Sept.

When flowering is over, fruit grows inside sepals (or calyx)

Calyx is smaller than that of Bladder Campion

◀ White Campion

The erect stems and the sepals are sticky and hairy. The white petals are divided. Look in hedgerows. Up to 1 m tall. May-June.

Corn Spurrey ▶

Spindly plant with jointed sticky stems. Narrow leaves in whorls around the stem. Weed of cornfields. 30 cm tall. April-July.

Whorl of leaves

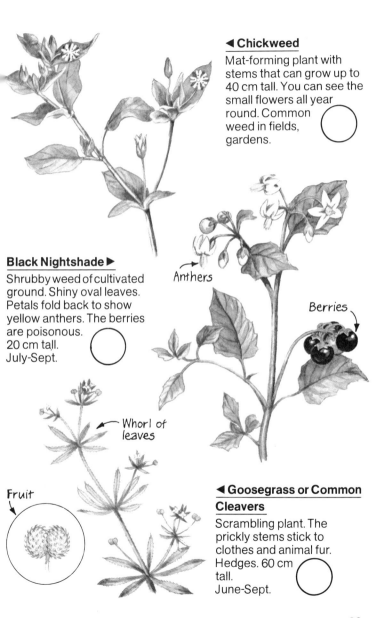

◀ Chickweed
Mat-forming plant with stems that can grow up to 40 cm tall. You can see the small flowers all year round. Common weed in fields, gardens.

Black Nightshade ▶
Shrubby weed of cultivated ground. Shiny oval leaves. Petals fold back to show yellow anthers. The berries are poisonous. 20 cm tall. July-Sept.

Anthers

Berries

Whorl of leaves

Fruit

◀ Goosegrass or Common Cleavers
Scrambling plant. The prickly stems stick to clothes and animal fur. Hedges. 60 cm tall. June-Sept.

Look for these flowers in grassy places, on waste or cultivated ground.

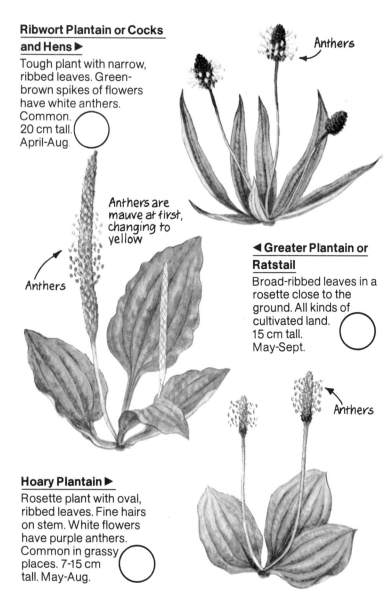

Ribwort Plantain or Cocks and Hens ▶

Tough plant with narrow, ribbed leaves. Green-brown spikes of flowers have white anthers. Common. 20 cm tall. April-Aug.

Anthers

Anthers are mauve at first, changing to yellow

Anthers

◀ Greater Plantain or Ratstail

Broad-ribbed leaves in a rosette close to the ground. All kinds of cultivated land. 15 cm tall. May-Sept.

Anthers

Hoary Plantain ▶

Rosette plant with oval, ribbed leaves. Fine hairs on stem. White flowers have purple anthers. Common in grassy places. 7-15 cm tall. May-Aug.

Look for these flowers on grassy or waste ground.

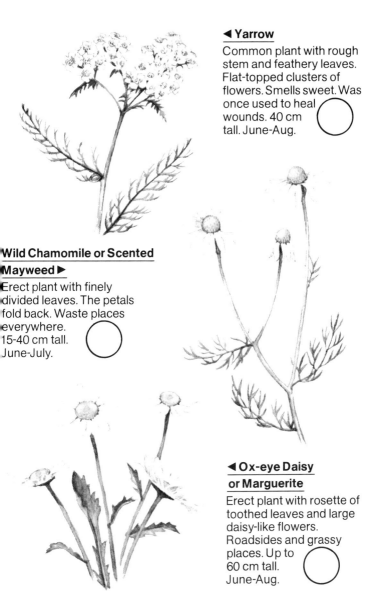

◄ Yarrow
Common plant with rough stem and feathery leaves. Flat-topped clusters of flowers. Smells sweet. Was once used to heal wounds. 40 cm tall. June-Aug.

Wild Chamomile or Scented Mayweed ►
Erect plant with finely divided leaves. The petals fold back. Waste places everywhere. 15-40 cm tall. June-July.

◄ Ox-eye Daisy or Marguerite
Erect plant with rosette of toothed leaves and large daisy-like flowers. Roadsides and grassy places. Up to 60 cm tall. June-Aug.

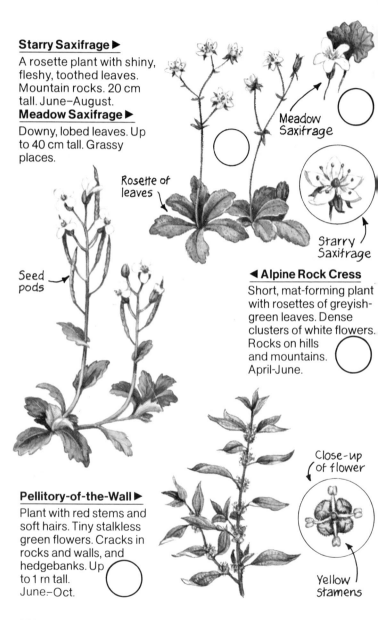

Starry Saxifrage ▶

A rosette plant with shiny, fleshy, toothed leaves. Mountain rocks. 20 cm tall. June–August.

Meadow Saxifrage ▶

Downy, lobed leaves. Up to 40 cm tall. Grassy places.

Meadow Saxifrage

Rosette of leaves

Starry Saxifrage

Seed pods

◀ Alpine Rock Cress

Short, mat-forming plant with rosettes of greyish-green leaves. Dense clusters of white flowers. Rocks on hills and mountains. April-June.

Pellitory-of-the-Wall ▶

Plant with red stems and soft hairs. Tiny stalkless green flowers. Cracks in rocks and walls, and hedgebanks. Up to 1 rn tall. June.-Oct.

Close-up of flower

Yellow stamens

102

Chapter 3
TREES

Introduction to Chapter 3

This chapter will help you to identify over 80 different trees. The chapter is arranged with conifers first, followed by broadleaved trees.

The illustrations show important features for identifying a tree at any time of the year. For each tree, the leaf, the bark, the shape of a full-grown tree in full leaf and its shape in winter (if the tree is deciduous) are shown. Flowers and fruits (including cones) are illustrated if they help in identification. The average height of a full-grown tree is written next to each illustration.

Remember that the shape of trees can vary a great deal. The Noble Fir that you spot, for example, may not have the same type of crown as the one shown on page 114. This is because young trees often look very different from middle-aged or mature trees of the same species. In this chapter we have shown mainly mature trees.

Conifers and broadleaved trees

A tree is a plant that grows on a single, central woody stem. Trees are divided into two main groups: conifers and broadleaved trees. Most broadleaved trees are deciduous: they have broad flat leaves which they drop in winter. (Some common types of leaves are shown on page 61.) Their seeds are enclosed in fruits. Most conifers are evergreen, with narrow, needle-like or scaly leaves that stay on the tree throughout the winter. Their fruits are usually woody cones.

Fruits and seeds

Fruits contain the seeds that will grow into new trees. Broadleaved trees produce many different types of fruit, including nuts, berries, and fleshy fruits. A cone is the woody fruit of a conifer and is made up of many overlapping scales which hold the seeds.

Broadleaved

Laburnum seed pods

Bird Cherry Soft fruit

Conifers

Cone scale
seed

seed
Scale
bract

Holly berries

Bract

Oak acorn

Plane "bobble"

Identifying winter buds

In winter you can identify broadleaved trees by their winter buds.

English Oak: clusters of stout, light brown buds on rugged twigs.

Turkey Oak: clusters of small, brown, whiskered buds.

Red Oak: clusters of reddish-brown buds on grey-green twigs with large bud at the tip.

Ash: large black buds on silver-grey twigs.

Alder: stalked violet buds. Male catkins often present.

Rowan: large blackish end bud with tuft of white hairs.

Leaf scars

Sycamore: large green buds with dark-edged scales on stout, light brown twigs.

White Poplar: very small, orange-brown bud covered by white felty hairs on green twigs.

White Willow: slender buds enclosed in a single scale, close to pinkish downy twig.

Common Beech: spiky copper-brown buds sticking out from brown twigs.

Hornbeam: dull brown or green buds, close to greyish-brown twigs.

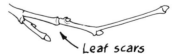

Leaf scars

London Plane: brown, cone-shaped buds with ring scars round them.

Common Lime: reddish-brown, lop-sided buds on reddish twigs.

Sweet Chestnut: rounded, reddish-brown buds on knobbly, greenish-brown twigs.

Conifers

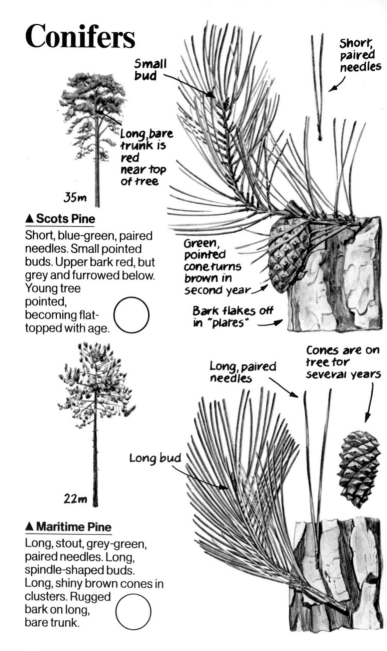

Small bud

Long, bare trunk is red near top of tree

35m

Short, paired needles

Green, pointed cone turns brown in second year

Bark flakes off in "plates"

▲ Scots Pine

Short, blue-green, paired needles. Small pointed buds. Upper bark red, but grey and furrowed below. Young tree pointed, becoming flat-topped with age.

22m

Long, paired needles

Cones are on tree for several years

Long bud

▲ Maritime Pine

Long, stout, grey-green, paired needles. Long, spindle-shaped buds. Long, shiny brown cones in clusters. Rugged bark on long, bare trunk.

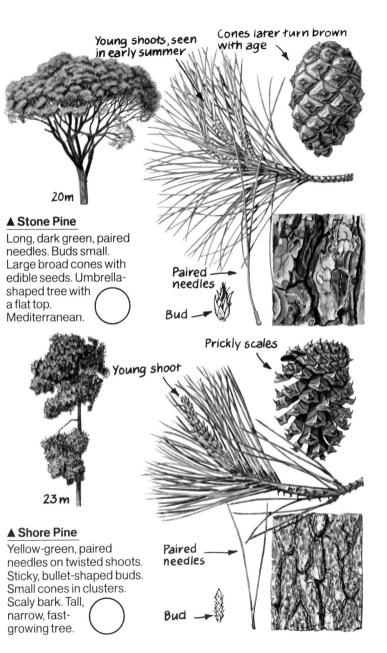

Young shoots, seen in early summer

Cones later turn brown with age

▲ Stone Pine

Long, dark green, paired needles. Buds small. Large broad cones with edible seeds. Umbrella-shaped tree with a flat top. Mediterranean.

20m

Paired needles

Bud

Prickly scales

Young shoot

▲ Shore Pine

Yellow-green, paired needles on twisted shoots. Sticky, bullet-shaped buds. Small cones in clusters. Scaly bark. Tall, narrow, fast-growing tree.

23 m

Paired needles

Bud

107

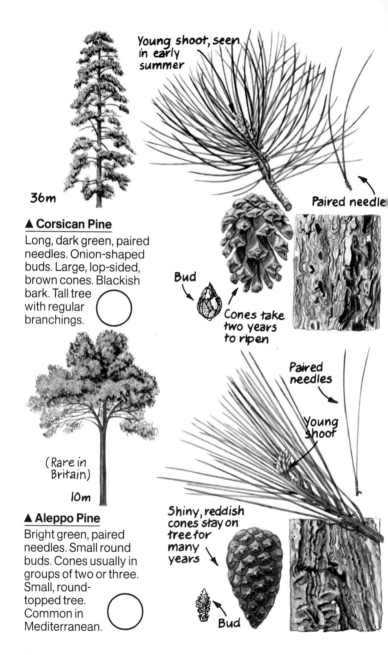

Young shoot, seen in early summer

36m

Paired needle

▲ Corsican Pine

Long, dark green, paired needles. Onion-shaped buds. Large, lop-sided, brown cones. Blackish bark. Tall tree with regular branchings.

Bud

Cones take two years to ripen

(Rare in Britain)

10m

Paired needles

Young shoot

▲ Aleppo Pine

Bright green, paired needles. Small round buds. Cones usually in groups of two or three. Small, round-topped tree. Common in Mediterranean.

Shiny, reddish cones stay on tree for many years

Bud

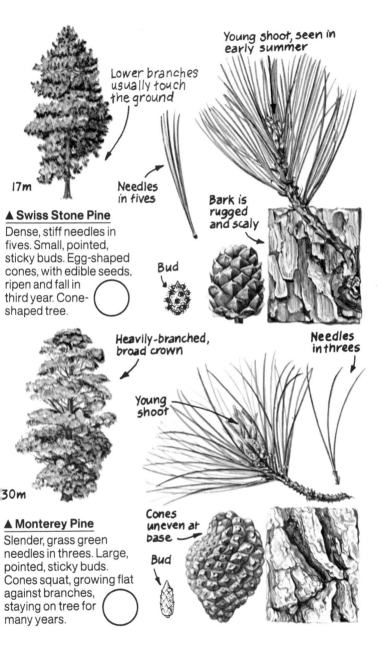

Young shoot, seen in early summer

Lower branches usually touch the ground

17m

Needles in fives

Bark is rugged and scaly

▲ Swiss Stone Pine
Dense, stiff needles in fives. Small, pointed, sticky buds. Egg-shaped cones, with edible seeds, ripen and fall in third year. Cone-shaped tree.

Bud

Heavily-branched, broad crown

Needles in threes

Young shoot

30m

▲ Monterey Pine
Slender, grass green needles in threes. Large, pointed, sticky buds. Cones squat, growing flat against branches, staying on tree for many years.

Cones uneven at base

Bud

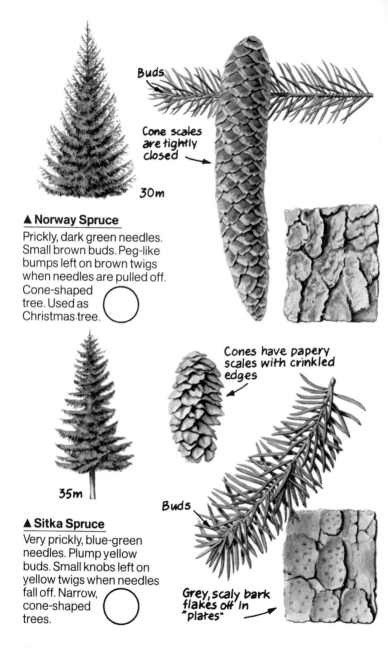

Buds

Cone scales are tightly closed

30m

▲ Norway Spruce

Prickly, dark green needles. Small brown buds. Peg-like bumps left on brown twigs when needles are pulled off. Cone-shaped tree. Used as Christmas tree.

Cones have papery scales with crinkled edges

35m

Buds

▲ Sitka Spruce

Very prickly, blue-green needles. Plump yellow buds. Small knobs left on yellow twigs when needles fall off. Narrow, cone-shaped trees.

Grey, scaly bark flakes off in "plates"

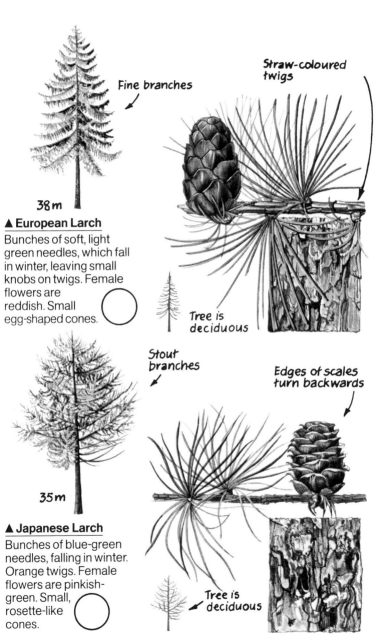

Fine branches

Straw-coloured twigs

38 m

▲ European Larch
Bunches of soft, light green needles, which fall in winter, leaving small knobs on twigs. Female flowers are reddish. Small egg-shaped cones.

Tree is deciduous

Stout branches

Edges of scales turn backwards

35 m

▲ Japanese Larch
Bunches of blue-green needles, falling in winter. Orange twigs. Female flowers are pinkish-green. Small, rosette-like cones.

Tree is deciduous

111

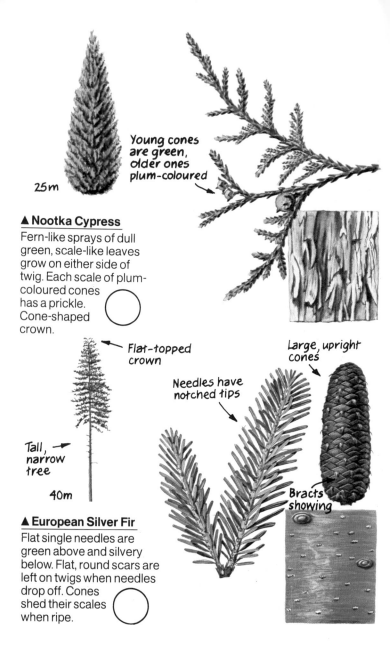

25m

Young cones
are green,
older ones
plum-coloured

▲ Nootka Cypress
Fern-like sprays of dull
green, scale-like leaves
grow on either side of
twig. Each scale of plum-
coloured cones
has a prickle.
Cone-shaped
crown.

Flat-topped
crown

Tall,
narrow
tree

40m

Large, upright
cones

Needles have
notched tips

Bracts
showing

▲ European Silver Fir
Flat single needles are
green above and silvery
below. Flat, round scars are
left on twigs when needles
drop off. Cones
shed their scales
when ripe.

▲ Greek Fir

Shiny green, spiny-tipped needles all round twig. Tall, narrow cones shed scales to leave bare spike on tree. Common in parks.

Pointed tip

Bark flakes off in "plates"

▲ Spanish Fir

Short, blunt, blue-grey needles all round twig. Cylindrical, upright cones fall apart on tree. Found only in gardens in Britain.

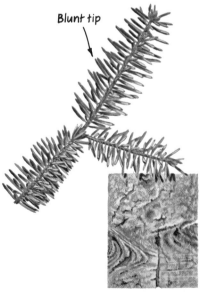

Blunt tip

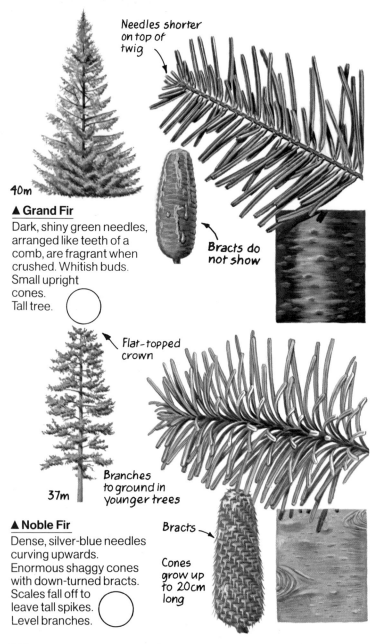

Needles shorter on top of twig

Bracts do not show

40m

▲ Grand Fir

Dark, shiny green needles, arranged like teeth of a comb, are fragrant when crushed. Whitish buds. Small upright cones. Tall tree.

Flat-topped crown

Branches to ground in younger trees

37m

▲ Noble Fir

Dense, silver-blue needles curving upwards. Enormous shaggy cones with down-turned bracts. Scales fall off to leave tall spikes. Level branches.

Bracts

Cones grow up to 20cm long

114

Beech-like bud

Needles are parted on twig

Bracts

▲ Douglas Fir
Soft fragrant needles. Long-pointed, copper-brown buds. Light brown, hanging cones with three-pointed bracts. Old bark is thick and corky.

Leader droops

Young cones are green, older ones are brown

Cone has a few rounded scales

Tips of branches droop

35m

▲ Western Hemlock
Needles various lengths, green above and silver below. Small cones on shoot tips. Smooth, brown scaly bark. Branch tips and top shoot droops.

Flattened needles

40m

115

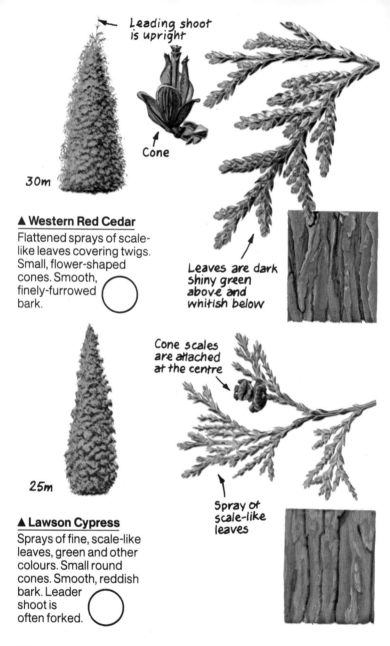

Leading shoot is upright

Cone

▲ Western Red Cedar
Flattened sprays of scale-like leaves covering twigs. Small, flower-shaped cones. Smooth, finely-furrowed bark.

Leaves are dark shiny green above and whitish below

Cone scales are attached at the centre

30m

25m

▲ Lawson Cypress
Sprays of fine, scale-like leaves, green and other colours. Small round cones. Smooth, reddish bark. Leader shoot is often forked.

Spray of scale-like leaves

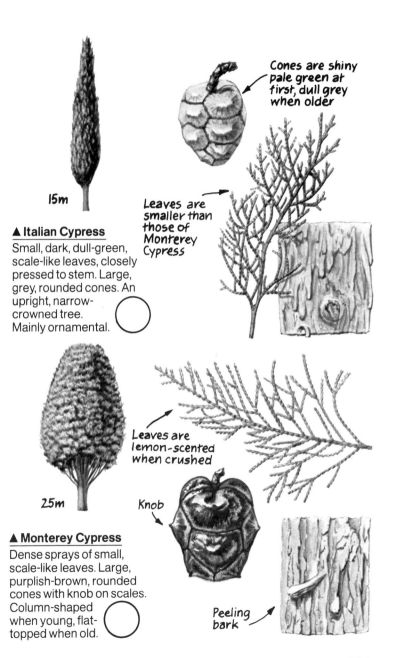

15m

Cones are shiny
pale green at
first, dull grey
when older

Leaves are
smaller than
those of
Monterey
Cypress

▲ Italian Cypress

Small, dark, dull-green,
scale-like leaves, closely
pressed to stem. Large,
grey, rounded cones. An
upright, narrow-
crowned tree.
Mainly ornamental.

25m

Leaves are
lemon-scented
when crushed

Knob

▲ Monterey Cypress

Dense sprays of small,
scale-like leaves. Large,
purplish-brown, rounded
cones with knob on scales.
Column-shaped
when young, flat-
topped when old.

Peeling
bark

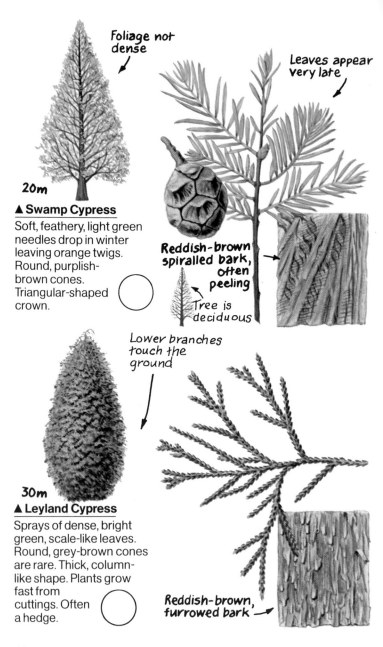

Foliage not
dense

Leaves appear
very late

20m
▲ Swamp Cypress
Soft, feathery, light green
needles drop in winter
leaving orange twigs.
Round, purplish-
brown cones.
Triangular-shaped
crown.

Reddish-brown
spiralled bark,
often
peeling

Tree is
deciduous

Lower branches
touch the
ground

30m
▲ Leyland Cypress
Sprays of dense, bright
green, scale-like leaves.
Round, grey-brown cones
are rare. Thick, column-
like shape. Plants grow
fast from
cuttings. Often
a hedge.

Reddish-brown,
furrowed bark

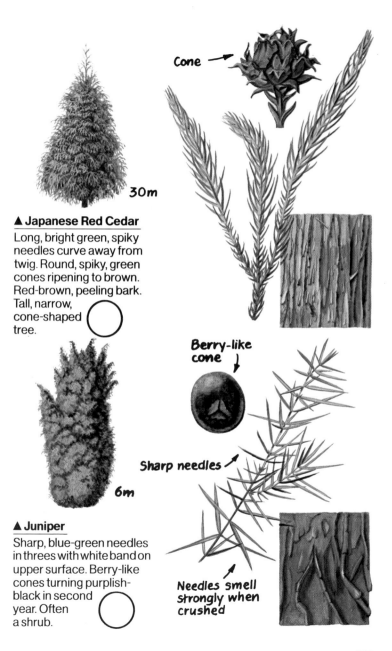

Cone

▲ Japanese Red Cedar

Long, bright green, spiky
needles curve away from
twig. Round, spiky, green
cones ripening to brown.
Red-brown, peeling bark.
Tall, narrow,
cone-shaped
tree.

30m

Berry-like cone

Sharp needles

6m

▲ Juniper

Sharp, blue-green needles
in threes with white band on
upper surface. Berry-like
cones turning purplish-
black in second
year. Often
a shrub.

Needles smell strongly when crushed

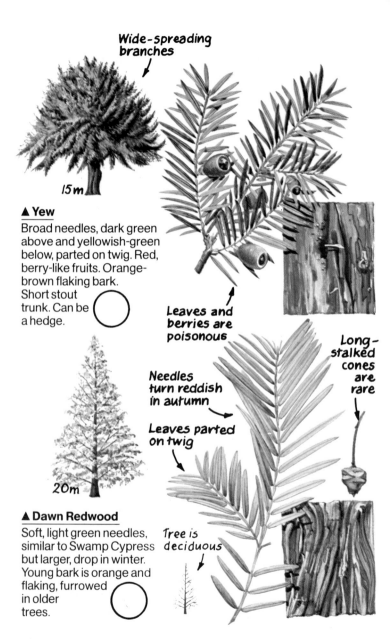

Wide-spreading branches

15m

▲ Yew
Broad needles, dark green above and yellowish-green below, parted on twig. Red, berry-like fruits. Orange-brown flaking bark. Short stout trunk. Can be a hedge.

Leaves and berries are poisonous

Needles turn reddish in autumn

Leaves parted on twig

Long-stalked cones are rare

20m

▲ Dawn Redwood
Soft, light green needles, similar to Swamp Cypress but larger, drop in winter. Young bark is orange and flaking, furrowed in older trees.

Tree is deciduous

▲ Coast Redwood

Hard, sharp-pointed needles, dark green above and white-banded below. Small, round cones. Thick, reddish, spongy bark. Tall tree.

Needles parted on either side of twig

▲ Wellingtonia

Deep green, scale-like, pointed leaves. Long-stalked, round, corky cones. Soft, thick, deeply-furrowed bark. Tall tree with upswept branches.

Foliage hanging from upswept branches

Diamond-shaped cone scales wrinkle when they ripen

121

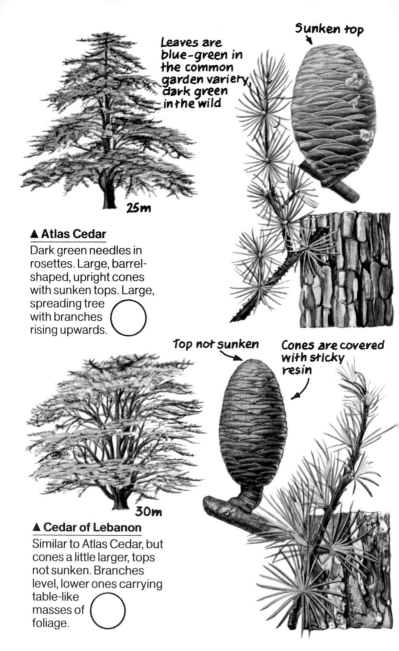

Leaves are blue-green in the common garden variety, dark green in the wild

Sunken top

▲ Atlas Cedar
Dark green needles in rosettes. Large, barrel-shaped, upright cones with sunken tops. Large, spreading tree with branches rising upwards.

Top not sunken

Cones are covered with sticky resin

25m

30m

▲ Cedar of Lebanon
Similar to Atlas Cedar, but cones a little larger, tops not sunken. Branches level, lower ones carrying table-like masses of foliage.

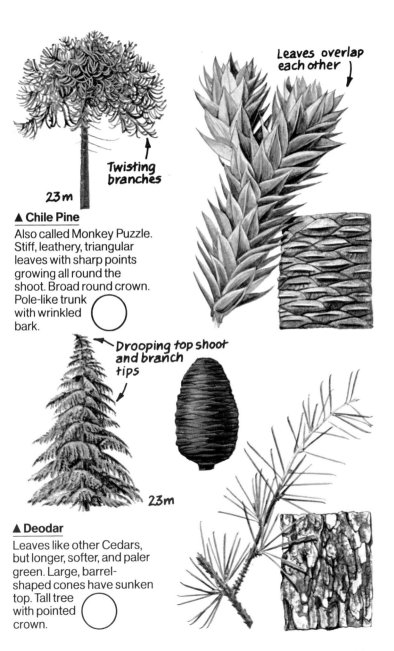

Leaves overlap each other

Twisting branches

23 m

▲ Chile Pine

Also called Monkey Puzzle. Stiff, leathery, triangular leaves with sharp points growing all round the shoot. Broad round crown. Pole-like trunk with wrinkled bark.

Drooping top shoot and branch tips

23m

▲ Deodar

Leaves like other Cedars, but longer, softer, and paler green. Large, barrel-shaped cones have sunken top. Tall tree with pointed crown.

Broadleaved Trees

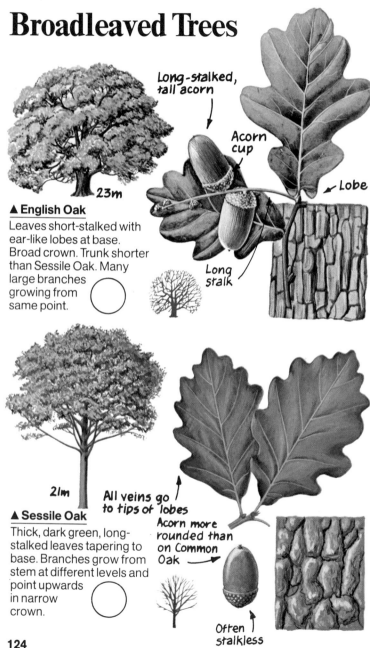

Long-stalked, tall acorn

Acorn cup

Lobe

▲ English Oak
Leaves short-stalked with ear-like lobes at base. Broad crown. Trunk shorter than Sessile Oak. Many large branches growing from same point.

23m

Long stalk

▲ Sessile Oak
Thick, dark green, long-stalked leaves tapering to base. Branches grow from stem at different levels and point upwards in narrow crown.

21m

All veins go to tips of lobes

Acorn more rounded than on Common Oak

Often stalkless

Leaf shape varies

Teeth

Evergreen leaves

Small acorn, almost covered by cup

▲ Holm Oak

Shiny evergreen leaves, greyish-green beneath, sometimes with shallow teeth like Holly leaves. Common ornamental tree. Broad dense crown.

20m

▲ Turkey Oak

Leaves unevenly lobed and saw-toothed. Whiskers on buds and at base of leaves. Acorn cups mossy and stalkless. Acorns ripen in second autumn.

25m

Acorn cup is mossy

▲ Cork Oak

Shiny evergreen leaves with wavy edge. Thick, corky, whitish bark. Small tree, except in warmer countries. Common in southern Europe.

Twisted trunk and branches

Acorn

Cork is obtained from the bark

Autumn colour of leaves

▲ Red Oak

Large leaves with bristly-tipped lobes, turn reddish-brown in autumn. Squat acorns in shallow cups ripen in second year. Smooth silvery bark.

Acorn

16m

20m

25m

▲ **Common Ash**
Compound leaf of 9-13 leaflets appearing late, after bunches of purplish flowers. Clusters of "keys" stay on the tree into winter. Pale grey bark.

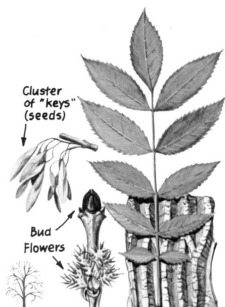

Cluster of "keys" (seeds)

Bud

Flowers

20m

▲ **Manna Ash**
Compound leaf of 5-9 stalked leaflets. Clusters of showy white flowers in May. Smooth grey bark oozes sugary liquid called manna.

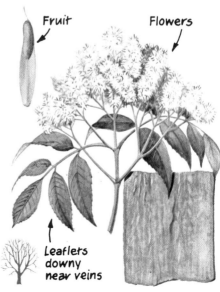

Fruit

Flowers

Leaflets downy near veins

Leaf has
notched tip

Cone-like
fruit stays on
all winter

▲ Common Alder
Leaves rounded, falling in
late autumn. Young twigs
and leaves sticky. Reddish
catkins. Fruits like small,
brown, woody
cones. Always
near water.

12m

Green fruits ripen
into brown, woody
"cones" (shown above)

▲ Grey Alder
Pointed oval leaves with
sharply-toothed edge, soft
and grey underneath.
Twigs and bark grey.
Catkins and fruit
like Common
Alder.

14m

Berries

One flower
(from a
cluster)

Toothed
edge

Leaves
turn red
in Autumn

7m

▲ Rowan

Compound leaf like Ash,
but smaller. Clusters of
creamy-white flowers in
May. Red berries ripen in
August. Small tree.
Often grows alone
on mountainsides.

8m

▲ Whitebeam

Large oval leaves with
toothed edge, white and
furry underneath. Flowers
and fruit like Rowan but
ripen later.
Grows at edges
of woods.

Berries

Leaf stalk is flattened →

20m

▲ Aspen

Rounded leaves with wavy edge, trembling in wind. White downy catkins. Grey bark with large pores. Smaller than other Poplars. Often in thickets.

Fan-shaped crown

25m

▲ Black Italian Poplar

Dark green, triangular, pointed leaves, appearing late. Red catkins. Deeply furrowed bark. Trunk and crown often lean away from wind. Grows fast.

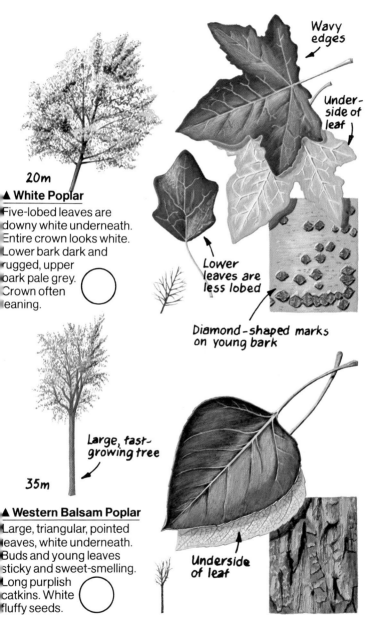

20m

▲ White Poplar

Five-lobed leaves are
downy white underneath.
Entire crown looks white.
Lower bark dark and
rugged, upper
bark pale grey.
Crown often
leaning.

Wavy
edges

Under-
side of
leaf

Lower
leaves are
less lobed

Diamond-shaped marks
on young bark

35m

Large, fast-
growing tree

▲ Western Balsam Poplar

Large, triangular, pointed
leaves, white underneath.
Buds and young leaves
sticky and sweet-smelling.
Long purplish
catkins. White
fluffy seeds.

Underside
of leaf

131

Leaf shape varies

28m

▲ Lombardy Poplar
Pointed triangular leaves.
Tall narrow tree. Branches
grow upwards from
ground. Furrowed
bark. Often along
roadsides.

High-domed crown

Leaf from upper branch

23m

Rounded leaf from lower branch

▲ Grey Poplar
Similar to White Poplar.
Wavy-edged leaves, never
deeply lobed, downy white
underneath. Upper bark
yellowish-grey,
lower bark
dark, furrowed.

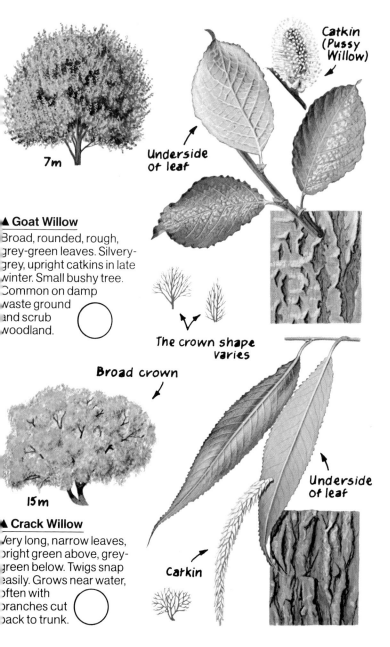

Catkin (Pussy Willow)

Underside of leaf

▲ Goat Willow

Broad, rounded, rough, grey-green leaves. Silvery-grey, upright catkins in late winter. Small bushy tree. Common on damp waste ground and scrub woodland.

7m

The crown shape varies

Broad crown

▲ Crack Willow

Very long, narrow leaves, bright green above, grey-green below. Twigs snap easily. Grows near water, often with branches cut back to trunk.

15m

Underside of leaf

Catkin

20m

▲ White Willow

Long, narrow, finely-toothed leaves, white underneath. Slender twigs, hard to break. Common by water. Weeping Willow is a variety with trailing branches.

Underside of leaf →

Catkin ↓

15m

▲ Silver Birch

Small, diamond-shaped leaves with double-toothed edge. Long "lamb's tail" catkins in April. Slender tree with drooping branches.

Catkin

Silvery bark peels off in ribbons →

Leaves are wavy-edged

▲ Common Beech

Light green, oval leaves
turn copper-brown in
autumn. Triangular nuts
in hairy husks. Tall tree
with spreading
crown. Smooth
grey bark.

Nuts in husk

▲ Hornbeam

Sharply-toothed, oval
leaves. In autumn, clusters
of three-pronged, leaf-
like wings hold nuts.
Smooth grey bark
is fluted (or
rippled).

Cluster of green winged fruits

135

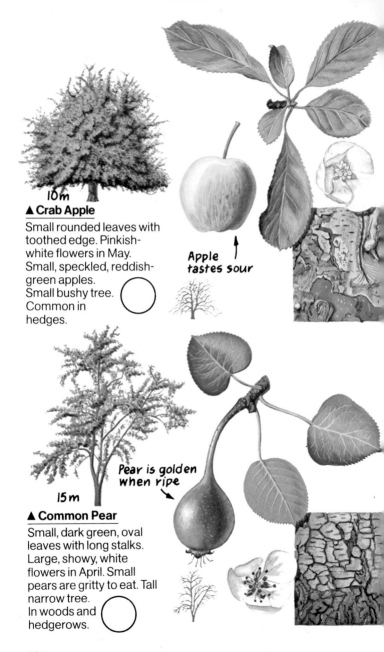

10m

▲ Crab Apple

Small rounded leaves with toothed edge. Pinkish-white flowers in May. Small, speckled, reddish-green apples. Small bushy tree. Common in hedges.

Apple tastes sour

15m

▲ Common Pear

Small, dark green, oval leaves with long stalks. Large, showy, white flowers in April. Small pears are gritty to eat. Tall narrow tree. In woods and hedgerows.

Pear is golden when ripe

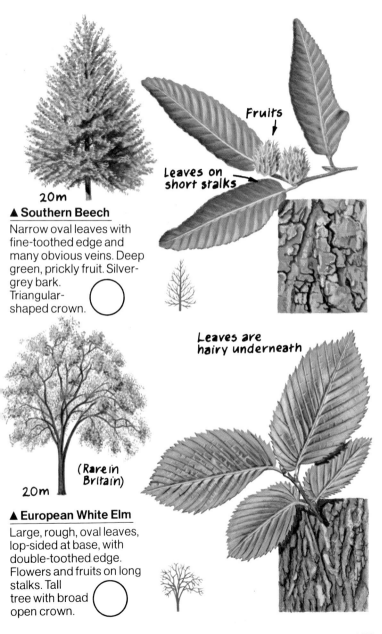

20m

▲ Southern Beech

Narrow oval leaves with fine-toothed edge and many obvious veins. Deep green, prickly fruit. Silver-grey bark. Triangular-shaped crown.

Fruits

Leaves on short stalks

Leaves are hairy underneath

(Rare in Britain)

20m

▲ European White Elm

Large, rough, oval leaves, lop-sided at base, with double-toothed edge. Flowers and fruits on long stalks. Tall tree with broad open crown.

30m

▲ London Plane

Large broad leaves with pointed lobes. Spiny "bobble" fruits hanging all winter. Flaking bark leaving yellowish patches. Tall tree, often in towns.

Fruit

20m

▲ Sycamore

Dark green, leathery leaves with five lobes. Paired, closely-angled, winged seeds. Large spreading tree. Smooth brown bark becoming scaly.

Toothed edge

Seeds twist as they fall

Leaves turn golden in autumn

15m

▲ Norway Maple

Light green, thin leaves. Lobes and teeth are bristle-tipped. Paired seeds form wide angle. Smaller, less spreading than Sycamore. Finely-furrowed, grey bark.

Pairs of seeds spin as they fall

Lobes are blunt

Leaves turn golden in autumn

10m

▲ Field Maple

Small, dark green leaves with five lobes. Small, reddish, winged seeds form a straight line. Small tree with round head. Often in hedges.

Seeds

Broad crown

Leafy wing

Fruits

25m

▲ Common Lime

Heart-shaped leaves with toothed edge. Yellowish-green, sweet-smelling flowers in July. Small, round, hard, grey-green fruits hang from leafy wing.

Pointed tip

Rounded crown

Leafy wing

Fruits

20m

▲ Silver Lime

Very similar to Common Lime, but leaves dark green above, silvery-grey and hairy underneath. Crown more rounded than Common Lime.

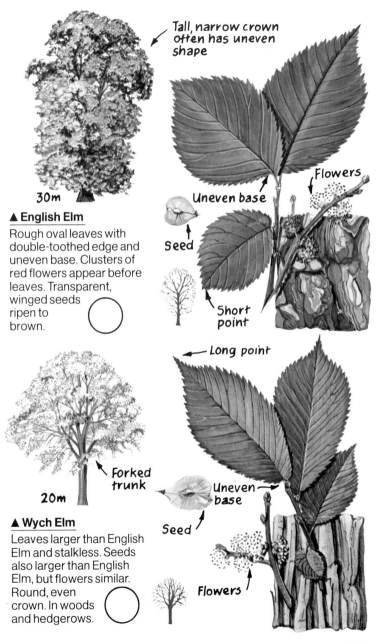

Tall, narrow crown
often has uneven
shape

Flowers

Uneven base

Seed

Short
point

▲ English Elm

Rough oval leaves with
double-toothed edge and
uneven base. Clusters of
red flowers appear before
leaves. Transparent,
winged seeds
ripen to
brown.

30m

Long point

Uneven base

Seed

Forked
trunk

20m

Flowers

▲ Wych Elm

Leaves larger than English
Elm and stalkless. Seeds
also larger than English
Elm, but flowers similar.
Round, even
crown. In woods
and hedgerows.

141

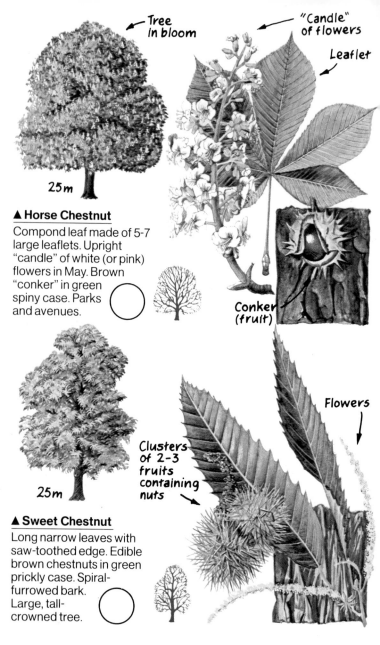

Tree
in bloom

"Candle"
of flowers

Leaflet

25m

▲ Horse Chestnut

Compond leaf made of 5-7
large leaflets. Upright
"candle" of white (or pink)
flowers in May. Brown
"conker" in green
spiny case. Parks
and avenues.

Conker
(fruit)

25m

▲ Sweet Chestnut

Long narrow leaves with
saw-toothed edge. Edible
brown chestnuts in green
prickly case. Spiral-
furrowed bark.
Large, tall-
crowned tree.

Clusters
of 2-3
fruits
containing
nuts

Flowers

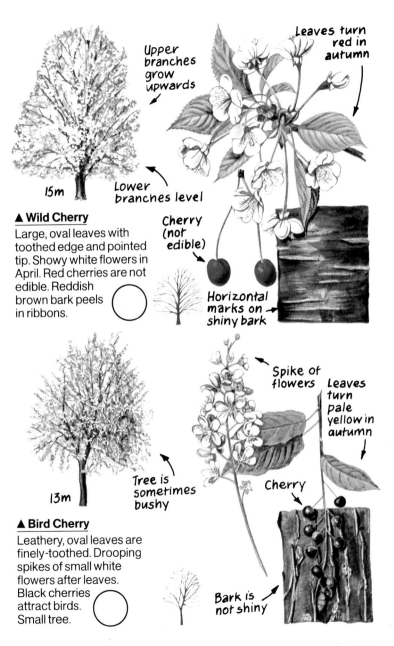

Upper branches grow upwards

Lower branches level

Leaves turn red in autumn

15m

▲ Wild Cherry

Large, oval leaves with toothed edge and pointed tip. Showy white flowers in April. Red cherries are not edible. Reddish brown bark peels in ribbons.

Cherry (not edible)

Horizontal marks on shiny bark

Spike of flowers

Leaves turn pale yellow in autumn

Tree is sometimes bushy

13m

▲ Bird Cherry

Leathery, oval leaves are finely-toothed. Drooping spikes of small white flowers after leaves. Black cherries attract birds. Small tree.

Cherry

Bark is not shiny

143

Unripe fruit

Ripe fruit

Young fruits

▲ Black Mulberry

Rough, heart-shaped leaves with toothed edge. Short catkins. Edible, blackish-red berries. Low, broad-crowned tree. Short trunk and twisted branches.

12m

Old trees have branches to the ground and often lean over

Smooth, green case containing edible walnut

Young fruit

▲ Common Walnut

Compound leaves of 7-9 untoothed leaflets. Twigs are hollow, with cross-sections inside. Smooth grey bark with some cracks, or fissures. Broad crown.

15m

Leaves are bronze when they first open, turning green later

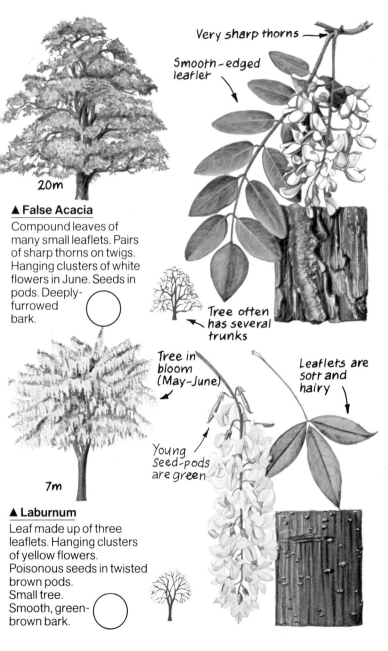

Very sharp thorns →

Smooth-edged leaflet

Tree often has several trunks

Leaflets are soft and hairy

Tree in bloom (May–June)

Young seed-pods are green

20m

▲ False Acacia

Compound leaves of many small leaflets. Pairs of sharp thorns on twigs. Hanging clusters of white flowers in June. Seeds in pods. Deeply-furrowed bark.

7m

▲ Laburnum

Leaf made up of three leaflets. Hanging clusters of yellow flowers. Poisonous seeds in twisted brown pods. Small tree. Smooth, green-brown bark.

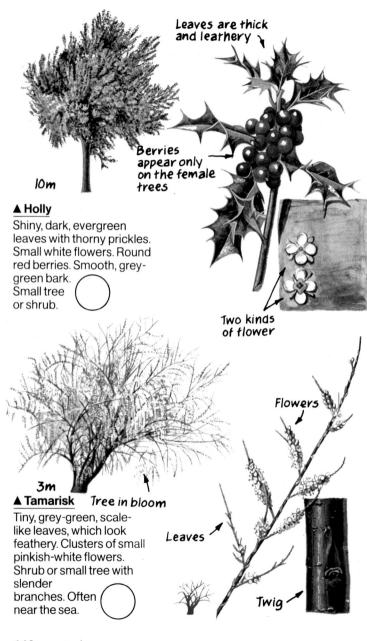

Leaves are thick
and leathery

Berries
appear only
on the female
trees

10m

▲ Holly

Shiny, dark, evergreen
leaves with thorny prickles.
Small white flowers. Round
red berries. Smooth, grey-
green bark.
Small tree
or shrub.

Two kinds
of flower

3m

▲ Tamarisk Tree in bloom

Tiny, grey-green, scale-
like leaves, which look
feathery. Clusters of small
pinkish-white flowers.
Shrub or small tree with
slender
branches. Often
near the sea.

Flowers

Leaves

Twig

▲ Common Olive

Narrow evergreen leaves in pairs. Clusters of small whitish flowers. Fleshy green fruit ripens to black. Small tree with twisted trunk.

Edible fruits are oily with hard stones

10m

(Not in Britain)

Tall trunk only in planted trees

4m

(Rare in Britain)

▲ European Fan Palm

Large, fan-shaped leaves made up of 12-15 stiff, pointed parts. Large clusters of small flowers and fruits. Wild plants form trunkless clumps of leaves.

Hairy trunk

Cone-like fruit

Squared lobe

20m

▲ Tulip Tree

Smooth, four-lobed leaves, golden in autumn. Large tulip-like flowers in June. Upright, brown, cone-like fruits. Tall, narrow-crowned tree.

Flower

Cleft

Maidenhair Tree is neither a conifer nor a broadleaved tree. It is in a group on its own

23m

▲ Maidenhair Tree

Double-lobed, fan shaped leaves with deep cleft, bright yellow in autumn. Hanging fruit on female trees. Male trees more common. Tall slender tree.

Fruit looks like a small plum

148

Chapter 4
FISHES

Introduction to Chapter 4

This chapter is a guide to some of the freshwater and sea fishes of Britain and Europe. The chapter is arranged with freshwater fishes first, followed by sea fishes. The fishes are also grouped according to their habitat.

The description next to each illustration gives information on where the fish lives, what it eats and where it spawns. It also gives the normal maximum length of an adult fish measured from head to tail. Given good conditions fishes can continue growing throughout their lives. The ones you will see or find may therefore be any size up to this maximum, depending on the age of the fish and its food supply.

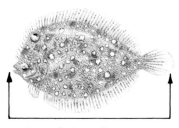

Length in metres
or centimetres

Parts of a fish

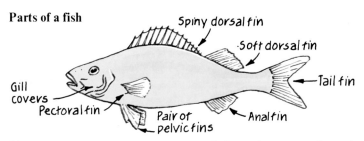

Spiny dorsal fin
Soft dorsal fin
Tail fin
Anal fin
Pair of pelvic fins
Pectoral fin
Gill covers

The pointed, torpedo-like shape of most fishes is good for moving through water. A fish swims by moving its tail fin and the back part of its body. The other fins help it to keep its balance. Most fishes have a swim bladder which helps to keep them buoyant.

Fishes take oxygen from the water by passing the water through their gills. They gulp water through their mouths with the gill covers closed. The gill covers then open and the water flows out through the gills.

Fishes are vertebrates; they have a backbone made up of many small bones called vertebrae. Their fins are made of bony material called rays. Most fishes are cold blooded; their body temperature changes with the temperature of the water. Most of them lay eggs and do not give birth to live young.

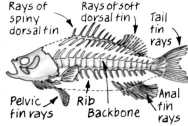

Rays of spiny dorsal fin
Rays of soft dorsal fin
Tail fin rays
Pelvic fin rays
Rib
Backbone
Anal fin rays

Camouflage

A fish with a good camouflage is hard to see against its background and is therefore difficult for an enemy to find.

The most common disguise for surface and midwater fishes is "counter shading". This means a dark back and a light or silvery belly and sides. Seen from above, by other fishes and by sea birds, the fish blends with the darkness of the water. Seen from below or from the side, the silver reflects the colour of the water and the fish becomes almost invisible.

Some fishes have stripes, spots or a strange shape which break up the normal outline of the body and confuse enemies. The dark colour or pattern of bottom-living fishes blends in with the mud, sand or stones of their background.

Mackerel
Counter shading. Ripple marking breaks up the outline of the back.

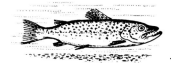

Sea Trout
Spots break up its outline, so it is hard to see against a stony bottom.

Worm Pipefish
Hides among seaweeds and pretends to be one of the stems.

Flounder
Can change its pattern and colour to match any surface it is lying on.

Anchovy
Swims in schools. When schools move the flashing sides of the fishes confuse enemies.

Pearlfish   Backbone visible
Its body is transparent and so is very difficult to see.

Butterfish
A row of spots along its back look like eyes and confuse enemies.

Shanny
Colour and pattern match colour and pattern of rocks and seaweeds.

Hill streams and highland lakes

The water is usually clear, cold and fast-flowing. The fishes shelter behind or under rocks. In lakes, many of the fishes spend the winter in deep water and eat very little.

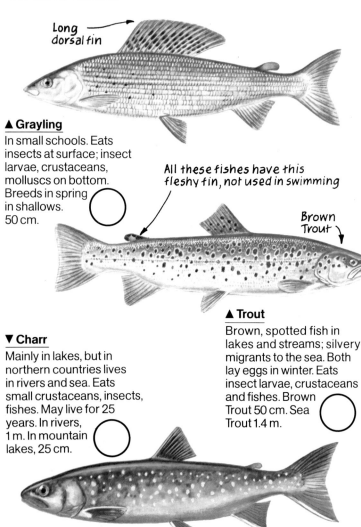

Long dorsal fin

▲ Grayling
In small schools. Eats insects at surface; insect larvae, crustaceans, molluscs on bottom. Breeds in spring in shallows. 50 cm.

All these fishes have this fleshy fin, not used in swimming

Brown Trout

▼ Charr
Mainly in lakes, but in northern countries lives in rivers and sea. Eats small crustaceans, insects, fishes. May live for 25 years. In rivers, 1 m. In mountain lakes, 25 cm.

▲ Trout
Brown, spotted fish in lakes and streams; silvery migrants to the sea. Both lay eggs in winter. Eats insect larvae, crustaceans and fishes. Brown Trout 50 cm. Sea Trout 1.4 m.

Hill streams and highland lakes

Fleshy fin

▲ Powan

Mostly in mountain lakes, but found in rivers around the Baltic Sea. Feeds on small crustaceans. In rivers, 70 cm. In mountain lakes, 20 cm.

▼ Minnow

Large schools near surface often in shallow water. Eats insects, their larvae, crustaceans. 8 cm.

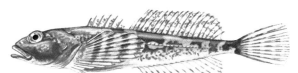

Male in breeding colours

▲ Bullhead

Hides under rocks and in dense plant growth by day. Active at dusk and dawn. Lays its eggs in a cavity under a large stone. 10 cm.

▼ Streber

Bottom-living, mainly solitary fish. Found in eastern Europe. Lives in fast-flowing streams. Eats insect larvae and crustaceans, mainly at night. 15 cm.

Middle reaches of rivers

The water current is moderate with fast-flowing stretches and also slower deep pools. The water is fairly clear and there are lots of water plants.

Sucker

Seven gill openings

▲ Lampern

Spawns in gravelly shallows. Young live in small streams, buried in mud. Migrates to sea to feed on other fishes by sucking their blood.
50 cm.

▼ Salmon

Migrates to Greenland to feed on shrimps and fishes, then returns to fresh water to lay its eggs in gravel streams in winter. Young stay in the river for up to three years. 1.5 m.

Fleshy fin

Salmon in river colours

Fleshy fin

▲ Rainbow Trout

North American fish introduced into Europe. Young eat insects, their larvae and crustaceans. Adults eat other fishes. 1 m.

Middle reaches of rivers

▲ Pike
Hides among water plants
waiting to attack prey.
Eats all but biggest fishes,
and sometimes ducklings and
water mammals.
Lives up to 20
years. 1.3 m.

▼ Dace
Likes moderate current and
clean shallow water. Usually
in schools. Eats insects at
the surface.
Spawns in gravelly
shallows. 30 cm.

▼ Chub
Forms schools when young,
but large fish live alone
in deep pools under trees
and river banks. Eats
fishes, insects
and crayfish.
50 cm.

*The shape of the anal fin
will help you tell the
difference between
Dace and Chub*

Bleak ▶
Lives at the surface of
the water in schools. Eats
water fleas and other
crustaceans, and
insects
on the
surface. 15 cm.

Anal fin

Middle reaches of rivers

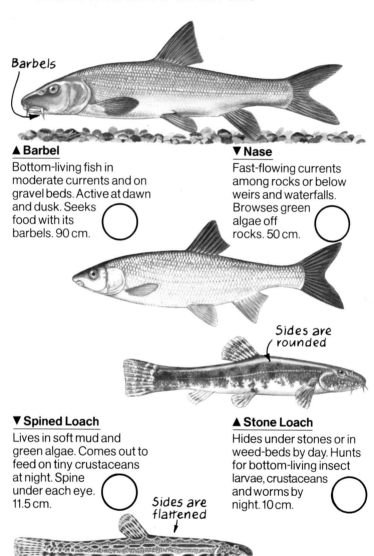

Barbels

▲ Barbel
Bottom-living fish in moderate currents and on gravel beds. Active at dawn and dusk. Seeks food with its barbels. 90 cm.

▼ Nase
Fast-flowing currents among rocks or below weirs and waterfalls. Browses green algae off rocks. 50 cm.

Sides are rounded

▼ Spined Loach
Lives in soft mud and green algae. Comes out to feed on tiny crustaceans at night. Spine under each eye. 11.5 cm.

Sides are flattened

▲ Stone Loach
Hides under stones or in weed-beds by day. Hunts for bottom-living insect larvae, crustaceans and worms by night. 10 cm.

Middle reaches of rivers

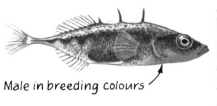

Male in breeding colours

◀ Stickleback
Lives in rivers, lakes and ponds; in the sea too in northern Europe. Feeds on small crustaceans. Makes nest close to the bottom. The male guards the eggs.
5 cm.

▲ Ruffe
Forms small schools close to the bottom. Feeds on insect larvae (bloodworms) and crustaceans. Lives for up to five years.
18 cm.

▼ Perch
Usually in large schools. Young lurk under bridges and landing stages; bigger ones live in deeper water. All eat smaller fishes and insect larvae. 51 cm.

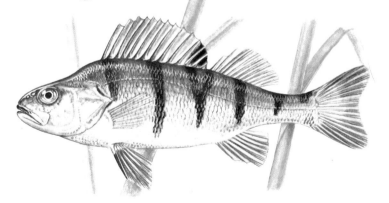

Lowland lakes and ponds

Mostly reservoirs, gravel-workings and farm ponds. Depending on size and age, the water varies from clear and well-oxygenated to coloured and stagnant. Usually full of plant and animal life. Fishes grow fast and large.

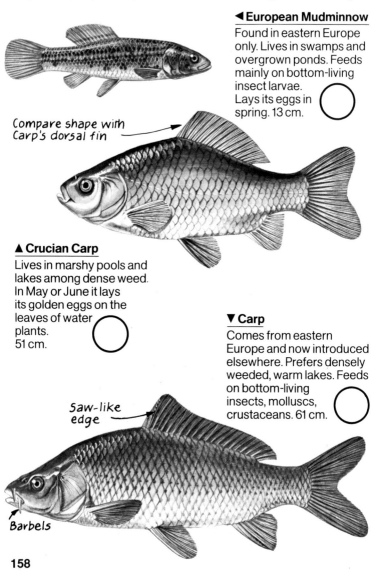

◀ European Mudminnow

Found in eastern Europe only. Lives in swamps and overgrown ponds. Feeds mainly on bottom-living insect larvae. Lays its eggs in spring. 13 cm.

Compare shape with Carp's dorsal fin

▲ Crucian Carp

Lives in marshy pools and lakes among dense weed. In May or June it lays its golden eggs on the leaves of water plants. 51 cm.

▼ Carp

Comes from eastern Europe and now introduced elsewhere. Prefers densely weeded, warm lakes. Feeds on bottom-living insects, molluscs, crustaceans. 61 cm.

Saw-like edge

Barbels

158

Lowland lakes and ponds

Angle of mouth
is steep

▲ Rudd
Lives in overgrown ponds
as well as lakes. Forms
schools. Feeds on surface-
living insects, as
well as larvae
and plants. 40 cm.

▼ Tench
Lives in dense weed-beds.
Burrows in mud in winter.
Eats insect larvae, snails,
crustaceans, and
occasionally
plants. 50 cm.

▲ Weatherfish
Often lives in overgrown
stagnant ponds. Gulps for
air at the surface. Becomes
restless in thundery
weather. Northern
and eastern
Europe only. 15 cm.

▼ Nine-spined Stickleback
In dense weed-beds, and
can live even in ditches.
Male makes a nest just off
the bottom. He
guards the eggs.
7 cm.

There can be 7 to 12
spines on the back

Male in
breeding colours

Lowland rivers

Usually slow-flowing with a gentle slope, winding through flat land.
Fishes prefer clouded water, little current and muddy bottoms.
Dense weed beds at edges provide food, shelter and places to spawn.
Often slightly polluted.

Lower jaw
sticks out

▲ Whitefish
In mountain lakes in
Britain and the Alps; in
rivers in northern Europe;
and in Baltic Sea. Eats
mainly fishes and
crustaceans.
Lakes, 25 cm.
Rivers, 35 cm.

▼ Goldfish
Comes from China and
Japan and now widespread
in Europe where pet fish
have escaped. In dense
weed where it
spawns in June
and July. 30 cm.

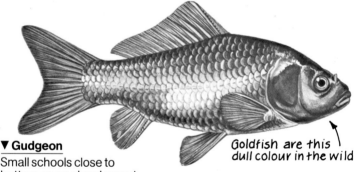

▼ Gudgeon
Small schools close to
bottom on mud and gravel
Uses long barbels to find
snails, crustaceans
and insect
larvae.
15 cm.

Goldfish are this
dull colour in the wild

Lowland rivers

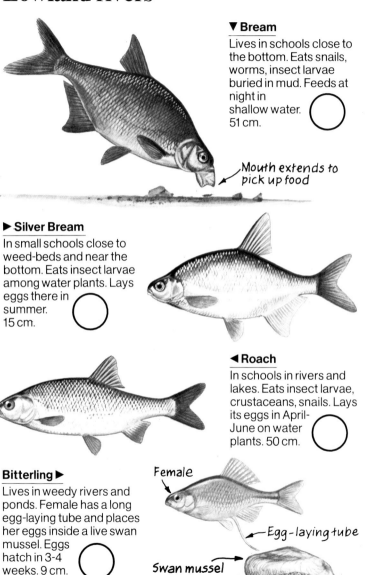

▼ Bream
Lives in schools close to the bottom. Eats snails, worms, insect larvae buried in mud. Feeds at night in shallow water. 51 cm.

Mouth extends to pick up food

▶ Silver Bream
In small schools close to weed-beds and near the bottom. Eats insect larvae among water plants. Lays eggs there in summer. 15 cm.

◀ Roach
In schools in rivers and lakes. Eats insect larvae, crustaceans, snails. Lays its eggs in April-June on water plants. 50 cm.

Bitterling ▶
Lives in weedy rivers and ponds. Female has a long egg-laying tube and places her eggs inside a live swan mussel. Eggs hatch in 3-4 weeks. 9 cm.

Female

Egg-laying tube

Swan mussel

161

Lowland rivers

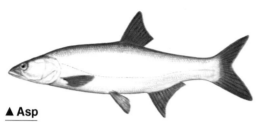

▲ Asp
Prefers moderate currents
but will live in lakes.
Young form schools; adults
mainly solitary. Sweden
and Germany
eastwards.
60 cm.

▼ Wels
The only native European
catfish. In deep, still
water. Hunts mainly at
night. Eats mostly
fishes, ducklings,
frogs. Rare. 3 m.

Barbels

Raised
nostrils ↘

▼ Zander
Comes from central
Europe but now spread
throughout northern
Europe. Found in schools
in cloudy water. Eats
smaller fish
mainly at dawn
and dusk. 70 cm.

▲ Burbot
Only member of the cod
family living in fresh water
Under tree roots and
holes in banks. Active
mainly at night.
Extinct in
Britain. 51 cm.

River mouths and estuaries

Water is fresh upstream and salty at the mouth. Fresh water often runs downstream above the sea water, which comes and goes with the tide. Usually muddy-bottomed with sand banks and few plants.

▲ Sea Lamprey

Eats larger fishes by sucking their blood. Migrates into fresh water to spawn, then adults die. Larvae spend three years buried in river mud. 91 cm.

▼ Sturgeon

Breeds in large rivers over gravel bottom. Migrates to sea to feed on bottom-living fishes, crustaceans, worms and molluscs. Now very rare and may die out completely. 3.5 m.

Yellow Eel

▲ Eel

Breeds in mid-Atlantic. Eel larva takes three years to float to Europe. Changes to an elver and swims upriver even into the tiniest streams. May live for 20 years in fresh water. 1 m.

▼ Twaite Shad

Large relative of the herring. Lives in the sea, but migrates up rivers to spawn on gravelly shallows. Eats crustaceans and small fishes. 55 cm.

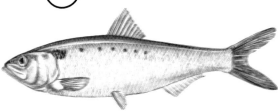

River mouths and estuaries

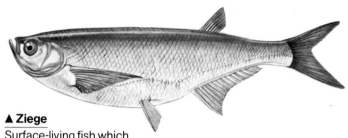

▲ Ziege
Surface-living fish which migrates in schools from the sea up rivers. Feeds mainly on fishes. Found in Baltic and Black Sea countries. 51 cm.

▼ European Toothcarp
In shallow pools at the sea's edge and in marshy estuaries. Eats small crustaceans and insect larvae. Mediterranean only. 5 cm.

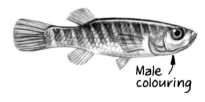

Male colouring

▼ Meagre
Uncommon in northern European seas, but elsewhere young are common in estuaries. Eats small fishes, and makes a loud rumbling sound as it hunts for food. 2 m.

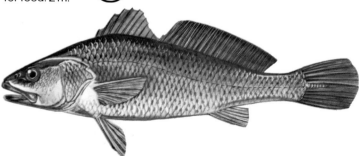

River mouths and estuaries

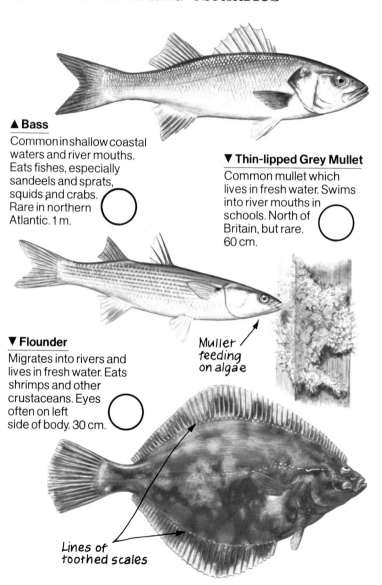

▲ Bass

Common in shallow coastal waters and river mouths. Eats fishes, especially sandeels and sprats, squids and crabs. Rare in northern Atlantic. 1 m.

▼ Thin-lipped Grey Mullet

Common mullet which lives in fresh water. Swims into river mouths in schools. North of Britain, but rare. 60 cm.

▼ Flounder

Migrates into rivers and lives in fresh water. Eats shrimps and other crustaceans. Eyes often on left side of body. 30 cm.

Mullet feeding on algae

Lines of toothed scales

Sandy beaches and shallow water

Many fishes burrow into the sand in shallow water and come out at high tide to look for food on the water-covered shore. Others live in schools, which gives them some protection, as there is no seaweed to hide in.

Greater Pipefish ▶

Common on muddy or sandy bottoms. Eats young fishes and tiny crustaceans. Male has a skin fold under his tail in which the eggs develop. 45 cm.

Barbels

▲ Five-bearded Rockling

Common in shallow water and on rocky shores. Young are silvery and live at the surface of the sea. Not in the Mediterranean. 25 cm.

Jellyfish

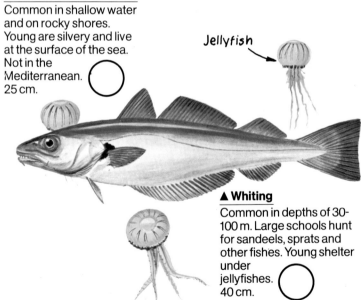

▲ Whiting

Common in depths of 30-100 m. Large schools hunt for sandeels, sprats and other fishes. Young shelter under jellyfishes. 40 cm.

Sandy beaches and shallow water

▲ Eelpout

Common fish on sandy and rocky shores in pools, under stones and algae. Gives birth to young about 4 cm long. North Atlantic only. 19 cm.

▲ Sand Smelt

Usually in huge schools. Breeds in shore pools in summer. Eggs have long threads which get tangled with seaweeds. 9 cm.

▼ Thick-lipped Grey Mullet

In coastal waters in large schools, migrating north in summer. Eats fine algae on rocks and on soft mud surface, which contains small animals. 75 cm.

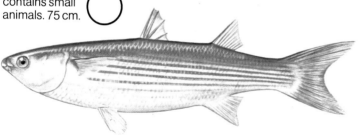

Hook

◄ Hooknose

Lives in shallow water 2-40 m deep. Often caught in shrimp nets. Feeds on small crustaceans, worms and molluscs. 20 cm.

Sandy beaches and shallow water

Lesser Weever ▶

Lies buried in sand in shallow water with its venomous spines sticking up. Feeds mostly on small shrimps and other crustaceans. DO NOT TOUCH. 14 cm.

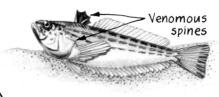

Venomous spines

▼ Sand Goby

Lives on sandy shores to 10 m deep. Eats small crustaceans and is often eaten by birds and fishes. Lays its eggs in a hollow shell. 9 cm.

▲ Sandeel

In huge schools close to the bottom. Burrows head-first in the sand. Eaten by other fishes and birds, like terns and puffins. Not in Mediterranean. 20 cm.

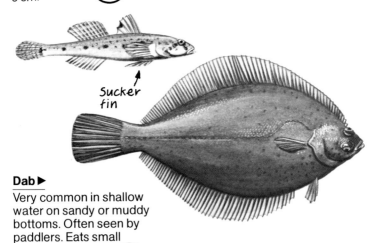

Sucker fin

Dab ▶

Very common in shallow water on sandy or muddy bottoms. Often seen by paddlers. Eats small crustaceans. Not in Mediterranean. 25 cm.

Rocky shores and shallow water

Rich in animal and plant life. Fishes live in pools, under stones or among seaweed. Many spend most of their lives on the same shore.

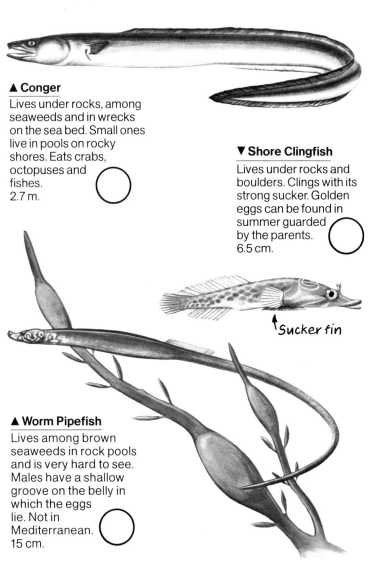

▲ Conger

Lives under rocks, among seaweeds and in wrecks on the sea bed. Small ones live in pools on rocky shores. Eats crabs, octopuses and fishes.
2.7 m.

▼ Shore Clingfish

Lives under rocks and boulders. Clings with its strong sucker. Golden eggs can be found in summer guarded by the parents.
6.5 cm.

Sucker fin

▲ Worm Pipefish

Lives among brown seaweeds in rock pools and is very hard to see. Males have a shallow groove on the belly in which the eggs lie. Not in Mediterranean.
15 cm.

Rocky shores and shallow water

Lower jaw
sticks out

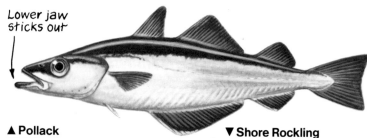

▲ Pollack

In schools in midwater, close to rocks when adult. Eats fishes, especially sandeels and herrings. Not in eastern Mediterranean. 1.3 m.

▼ Shore Rockling

Most common on rocky shores in pools and under seaweed. Its three barbels help it to locate shrimps, small crabs and worms, which it eats. 35 cm.

Barbels

Sea Scorpion ▶

Common fish in shore pools and among seaweeds. Eats shrimps, small crabs and fishes. Not in Mediterranean. 17 cm.

Flaps of skin help
camouflage fish

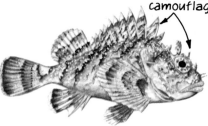

◀ Scorpionfish

Lies motionless among rocks and under seaweeds in shallow water. Hunts for crustaceans and fish at night. Not in north Atlantic. 25 cm.

Rocky shores and shallow water

14 to 16 spines ⟶

▲ Sea Stickleback
Lives entirely in the sea among seaweeds and eel-grass. Male builds a cup-sized nest in the seaweed. Not found in Mediterranean. 15 cm.

▼ Cardinalfish
In small groups in caves or crevices in rocky outcrops. Hunts actively at night. Male holds the eggs in his mouth until they hatch. Mediterranean only. 15 cm.

▼ Damselfish
Very common in Mediterranean. Forms large schools close to rocks. Lays its eggs on flat patches of rock. Male guards the eggs. 15 cm.

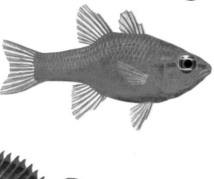

Rocky shores and shallow water

"Saddle"

◀ Saddled Bream
In small schools close to rocks often 2-3 m below the surface. Eats small bottom-living animals and seaweeds. Not in north Atlantic. 30 cm.

▼ Parrot Fish
Small groups swim around rocks. They scrape algae off rock with their strong teeth. Mediterranean only. 50 cm.

▲ Two-banded Bream
Common in small groups close to seaweed-covered rocks. Eats crustaceans and worms. Not in north Atlantic. 25 cm.

Broad teeth make mouth look like a parrot's beak

Goldsinny ▶
Lives close to seaweed-covered rocks and in eelgrass beds, occasionally in shore pools. 15 cm.

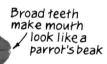

Rocky shores and shallow water

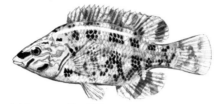

▲ Five-spotted Wrasse

In shallow water among rocks and seaweeds. Male makes large seaweed nest for female's eggs. He guards the eggs. Mediterranean only. 15 cm.

▼ Ocellated Wrasse

In Mediterranean at moderate depths near rocks and sand. Builds seaweed nest for its eggs. Eats parasites which live on the bodies of other fishes. 13 cm.

Colour varies

▲ Ballan Wrasse

Large wrasse. Common except in Mediterranean. Lives in loose schools around rocks. Feeds mainly on mussels. 60 cm.

▼ Cuckoo Wrasse

Rather uncommon wrasse. Lives near rocks. Male displays his bright colours to female before she will lay her eggs. 35 cm.

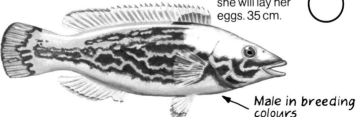

Male in breeding colours

Rocky shores and shallow water

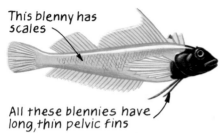

This blenny has scales

All these blennies have long, thin pelvic fins

◀ Black-faced Blenny

Found on rocky shores in shallow water where it basks in the sun. Male has a territory about 1 m wide which he defends. Only in Mediterranean. 8 cm.

Montagu's Blenny ▶

In rock pools almost bare of seaweeds. Eats acorn barnacles fastened to rocks, biting their limbs off when they come out from their shells. 8.5 cm.

One triangular flap on head

Other blennies have no scales

▲ Shanny

Very common shore fish in pools and among seaweeds on sandy and rocky shores. Eats small crustaceans. 16 cm.

▼ Peacock Blenny

Very shallow water on mud and sand near rocks. Lays eggs under empty shells or in hollows in rocks. Mediterranean only. 10 cm.

Rocky shores and shallow water

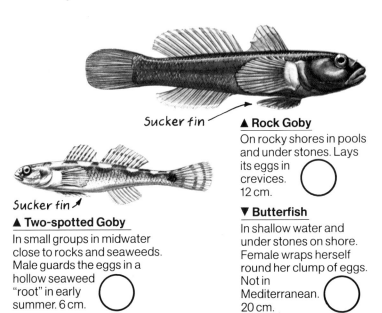

Sucker fin

Sucker fin

▲ Rock Goby
On rocky shores in pools
and under stones. Lays
its eggs in
crevices.
12 cm.

▲ Two-spotted Goby
In small groups in midwater
close to rocks and seaweeds.
Male guards the eggs in a
hollow seaweed
"root" in early
summer. 6 cm.

▼ Butterfish
In shallow water and
under stones on shore.
Female wraps herself
round her clump of eggs.
Not in
Mediterranean.
20 cm.

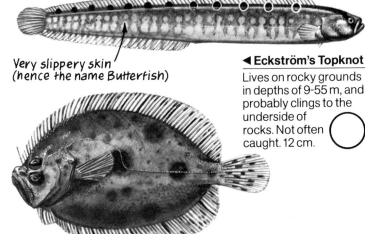

Very slippery skin
(hence the name Butterfish)

◀ Eckström's Topknot
Lives on rocky grounds
in depths of 9-55 m, and
probably clings to the
underside of
rocks. Not often
caught. 12 cm.

Inshore bottom-living fishes

Many of these fishes burrow or match their colouring to the sand on sandy bottoms. Others find food and shelter in rocky areas and wrecked ships.

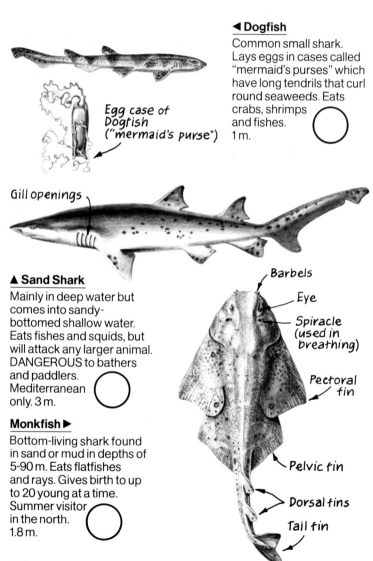

◀ Dogfish

Common small shark. Lays eggs in cases called "mermaid's purses" which have long tendrils that curl round seaweeds. Eats crabs, shrimps and fishes. 1 m.

Egg case of Dogfish ("mermaid's purse")

Gill openings

▲ Sand Shark

Mainly in deep water but comes into sandy-bottomed shallow water. Eats fishes and squids, but will attack any larger animal. DANGEROUS to bathers and paddlers. Mediterranean only. 3 m.

Monkfish ▶

Bottom-living shark found in sand or mud in depths of 5-90 m. Eats flatfishes and rays. Gives birth to up to 20 young at a time. Summer visitor in the north. 1.8 m.

Barbels

Eye

Spiracle (used in breathing)

Pectoral fin

Pelvic fin

Dorsal fins

Tail fin

Inshore bottom-living fishes

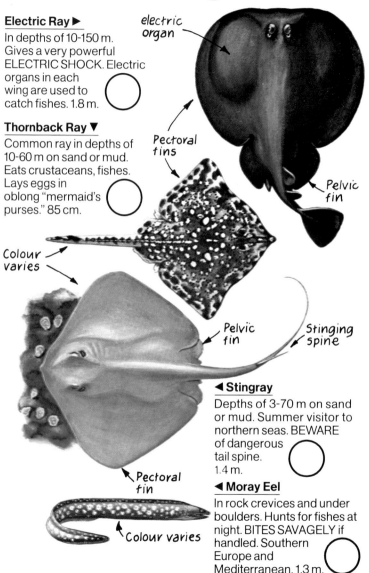

Electric Ray ▶

In depths of 10-150 m. Gives a very powerful ELECTRIC SHOCK. Electric organs in each wing are used to catch fishes. 1.8 m.

electric organ

Thornback Ray ▼

Common ray in depths of 10-60 m on sand or mud. Eats crustaceans, fishes. Lays eggs in oblong "mermaid's purses." 85 cm.

Pectoral fins

Pelvic fin

Colour varies

Pelvic fin

Stinging spine

◀ Stingray

Depths of 3-70 m on sand or mud. Summer visitor to northern seas. BEWARE of dangerous tail spine. 1.4 m.

Pectoral fin

◀ Moray Eel

In rock crevices and under boulders. Hunts for fishes at night. BITES SAVAGELY if handled. Southern Europe and Mediterranean. 1.3 m.

Colour varies

177

Inshore bottom-living fishes

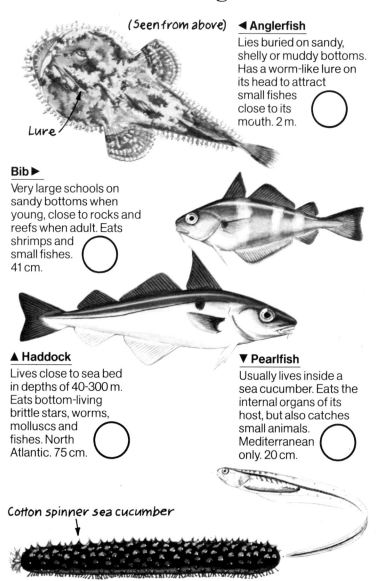

(Seen from above)

Lure

◀ Anglerfish
Lies buried on sandy, shelly or muddy bottoms. Has a worm-like lure on its head to attract small fishes close to its mouth. 2 m.

Bib ▶
Very large schools on sandy bottoms when young, close to rocks and reefs when adult. Eats shrimps and small fishes. 41 cm.

▲ Haddock
Lives close to sea bed in depths of 40-300 m. Eats bottom-living brittle stars, worms, molluscs and fishes. North Atlantic. 75 cm.

▼ Pearlfish
Usually lives inside a sea cucumber. Eats the internal organs of its host, but also catches small animals. Mediterranean only. 20 cm.

Cotton spinner sea cucumber

Inshore bottom-living fishes

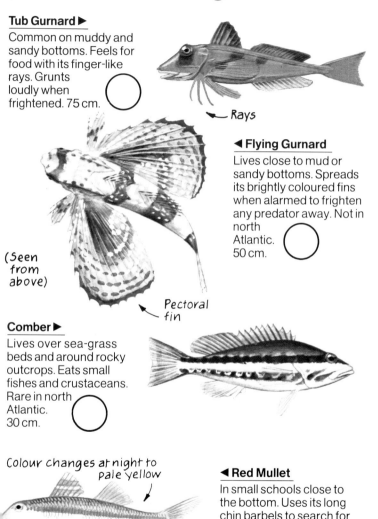

Tub Gurnard ▶
Common on muddy and
sandy bottoms. Feels for
food with its finger-like
rays. Grunts
loudly when
frightened. 75 cm.

← Rays

◀ Flying Gurnard
Lives close to mud or
sandy bottoms. Spreads
its brightly coloured fins
when alarmed to frighten
any predator away. Not in
north
Atlantic.
50 cm.

(Seen
from
above)

Pectoral
fin

Comber ▶
Lives over sea-grass
beds and around rocky
outcrops. Eats small
fishes and crustaceans.
Rare in north
Atlantic.
30 cm.

Colour changes at night to
pale yellow

◀ Red Mullet
In small schools close to
the bottom. Uses its long
chin barbels to search for
food. Young fish are silvery-
blue and live at
the surface of the
sea. 35 cm.

Barbels

179

Inshore bottom-living fishes

Red Band-fish ▶
Burrows in stiff mud in depths of 6-20 m. Comes out of its hole to snap up passing small crustaceans, and is occasionally eaten by other fishes. 50 cm.

Male

▲ Peacock Wrasse
Very common in the Mediterranean among weed-covered rocks at about 20 m. Females often change into males as they grow older. 20 cm.

▼ Rainbow Wrasse
Common in the Mediterranean close to rocks and in sea-grass beds. Lives in small schools led by the biggest male fish. Females change to males with age. 25 cm.

Adult male

Eyes

Small electric organs

▲ Stargazer
Lies buried in sand with only its eyes showing. Lures small fishes by vibrating its tongue. Detects them with weak electric currents. Mediterranean only. 25 cm.

Inshore bottom-living fishes

Butterfly Blenny ▶

Lives on shelly or rocky bottoms in depths of 10-100 m. Often "owns" a broken pot or hollow in which it lays its eggs in spring. 20 cm.

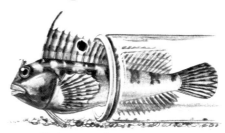

Male guarding nest in jar

▲ Wolf-fish

On rocky bottoms 20-300 m deep. Eats crabs, sea urchins and whelks. Crushes shells with its large teeth. North Atlantic only. 1.2 m.

▼ Dragonet

Near the bottom, 20-100 m deep. Often buries itself. Eats molluscs, crustaceans and worms. Male displays his long fins at spawning time. 20 cm.

Male

◀ Turbot

On gravel, shell and sandy bottoms in quite deep water. Eats bottom-living fishes like sandeels, dragonets and gobies. 80 cm.

181

Inshore bottom-living fishes

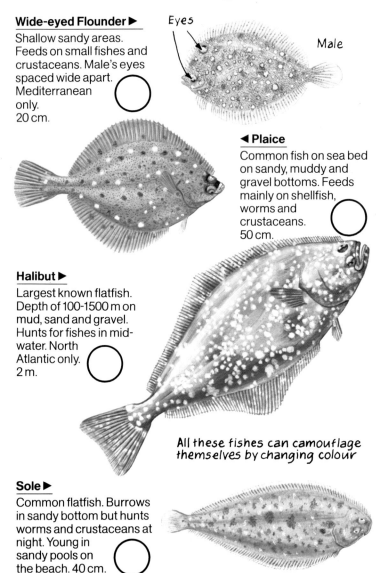

Wide-eyed Flounder ▶
Shallow sandy areas. Feeds on small fishes and crustaceans. Male's eyes spaced wide apart. Mediterranean only. 20 cm.

Eyes

Male

◀ Plaice
Common fish on sea bed on sandy, muddy and gravel bottoms. Feeds mainly on shellfish, worms and crustaceans. 50 cm.

Halibut ▶
Largest known flatfish. Depth of 100-1500 m on mud, sand and gravel. Hunts for fishes in mid-water. North Atlantic only. 2 m.

All these fishes can camouflage themselves by changing colour

Sole ▶
Common flatfish. Burrows in sandy bottom but hunts worms and crustaceans at night. Young in sandy pools on the beach. 40 cm.

Inshore midwater fishes

Most midwater fishes in inshore waters (up to 100 m deep) are schooling fishes. Only the largest fishes can live without the protection of a school.

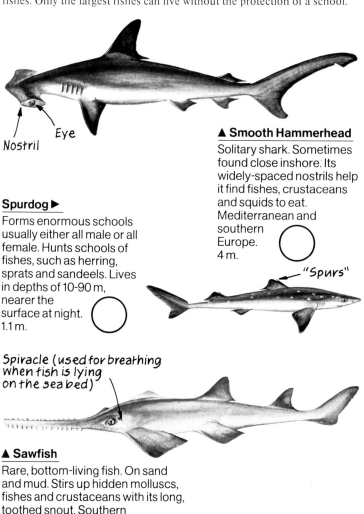

Eye

Nostril

▲ Smooth Hammerhead

Solitary shark. Sometimes found close inshore. Its widely-spaced nostrils help it find fishes, crustaceans and squids to eat. Mediterranean and southern Europe. 4 m.

"Spurs"

Spurdog ▶

Forms enormous schools usually either all male or all female. Hunts schools of fishes, such as herring, sprats and sandeels. Lives in depths of 10-90 m, nearer the surface at night. 1.1 m.

Spiracle (used for breathing when fish is lying on the sea bed)

▲ Sawfish

Rare, bottom-living fish. On sand and mud. Stirs up hidden molluscs, fishes and crustaceans with its long, toothed snout. Southern Europe and Mediterranean only. 4.5 m.

Inshore midwater fishes

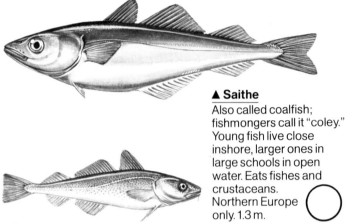

▲ Saithe

Also called coalfish;
fishmongers call it "coley."
Young fish live close
inshore, larger ones in
large schools in open
water. Eats fishes and
crustaceans.
Northern Europe
only. 1.3 m.

▲ Cod

Very common in midwater
and near sea bed. Large
schools. Eats many kinds
of fishes and
crustaceans.
Northern Europe
only. 1.2 m.

▼ Ling

Common fish around rocks
and wrecks as deep as
400 m. Eats mainly fishes
and crustaceans.
Not in the
Mediterranean.
2 m.

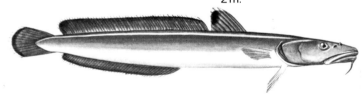

◀ Hake

Lives in quite deep water,
just above bottom, coming
nearer the surface at night.
Eats fishes and squids, and,
when young,
crustaceans.
1.8 m.

Inshore midwater fishes

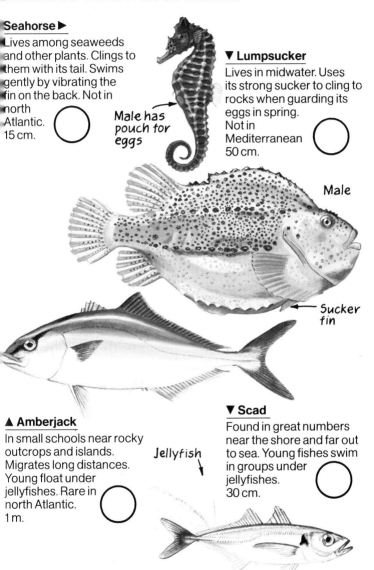

Seahorse ▶
Lives among seaweeds and other plants. Clings to them with its tail. Swims gently by vibrating the fin on the back. Not in north Atlantic. 15 cm.

Male has pouch for eggs

▼ Lumpsucker
Lives in midwater. Uses its strong sucker to cling to rocks when guarding its eggs in spring. Not in Mediterranean 50 cm.

Male

Sucker fin

▲ Amberjack
In small schools near rocky outcrops and islands. Migrates long distances. Young float under jellyfishes. Rare in north Atlantic. 1 m.

Jellyfish

▼ Scad
Found in great numbers near the shore and far out to sea. Young fishes swim in groups under jellyfishes. 30 cm.

185

Inshore midwater fishes

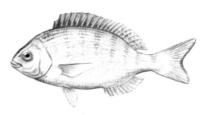

▼ Red Sea-bream
In schools when young, but adults form only small groups and live in deeper water (to 100 m). Eats fishes, crustaceans and squids. 50 cm.

▲ Black Sea-bream
Lives around wrecks and rocky outcrops close to sand. Hollows a nest in the sand for the eggs. The male guards them until they hatch. 35 cm.

▲ Saupe
Swims in close-packed schools in shallow water. Feeds by grazing fine algae off rocks and other seaweeds. Not in northern Europe. 30 cm.

◀ John Dory
Swims slowly. Lives alone. Lies in wait in the shadows for small fishes and snaps them up with its huge jaws. 40 cm.

Inshore surface fishes

Surface-living fishes are mostly plankton eaters (like the Mackerel) or fishes that hunt plankton eaters (like the Porbeagle Shark). Smaller fishes live in schools and most are silvery or white underneath and blue-green above.

Large gill openings

▲ Basking Shark
Largest fish in European seas but feeds on tiny plankton (larvae of crabs, molluscs and fishes). Hibernates in deep water in winter, probably on the sea bed. 11 m.

▼ Porbeagle
Active hunter of schools of fishes, such as herring, mackerel and pilchards, as well as squids. Gives birth to one or two well-developed young in summer. 3 m.

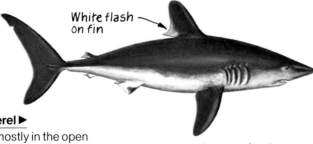

White flash on fin

Mackerel ▶
Lives mostly in the open sea often close to the surface. Eats surface-living crustaceans and young fishes, but in winter hibernates close to the sea bed. 40 cm.

This is a good example of "counter shading" (see page 53)

187

Inshore surface fishes

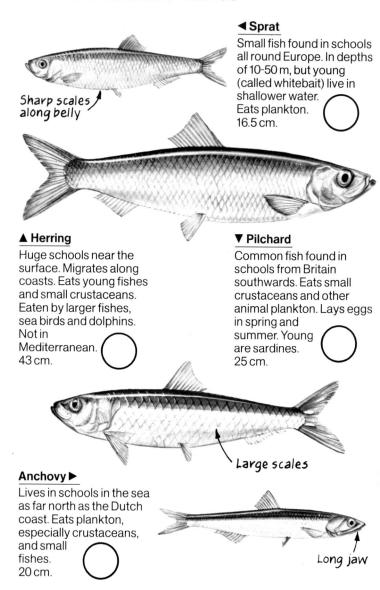

◄ Sprat
Small fish found in schools all round Europe. In depths of 10-50 m, but young (called whitebait) live in shallower water.
Eats plankton.
16.5 cm.

Sharp scales along belly

▲ Herring
Huge schools near the surface. Migrates along coasts. Eats young fishes and small crustaceans. Eaten by larger fishes, sea birds and dolphins. Not in Mediterranean.
43 cm.

▼ Pilchard
Common fish found in schools from Britain southwards. Eats small crustaceans and other animal plankton. Lays eggs in spring and summer. Young are sardines.
25 cm.

Large scales

Anchovy ►
Lives in schools in the sea as far north as the Dutch coast. Eats plankton, especially crustaceans, and small fishes.
20 cm.

Long jaw

Inshore surface fishes

▲ Garfish
Common at the sea's surface where it eats young fishes, like herrings and sandeels. Its eggs have long threads on their surface which tangle with floating seaweeds. 94 cm.

▼ Barracuda
Common in Mediterranean. Lives in large schools usually close to the surface. Hunts small fishes. 50 cm.

(Tropical Barracudas are very dangerous)

Spines can be locked in an upright position, so that the Triggerfish cannot be dragged out of rock crevices

▼ Triggerfish
In open sea and drifting with floating wreckage from the tropical Atlantic in summer. Eats crustaceans. 35 cm.

Ocean surface fishes

Most surface-living ocean fishes are blue-green above, white or silvery below. Many eat smaller, plankton-eating fishes which usually live in schools. Most migrate, moving into warmer water in winter.

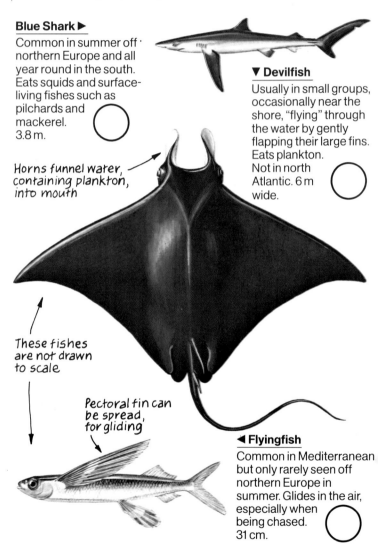

Blue Shark ▶

Common in summer off · northern Europe and all year round in the south. Eats squids and surface-living fishes such as pilchards and mackerel.
3.8 m.

▼ Devilfish

Usually in small groups, occasionally near the shore, "flying" through the water by gently flapping their large fins. Eats plankton. Not in north Atlantic. 6 m wide.

Horns funnel water, containing plankton, into mouth

These fishes are not drawn to scale

Pectoral fin can be spread, for gliding

◀ Flyingfish

Common in Mediterranean but only rarely seen off northern Europe in summer. Glides in the air, especially when being chased.
31 cm.

Ocean surface fishes

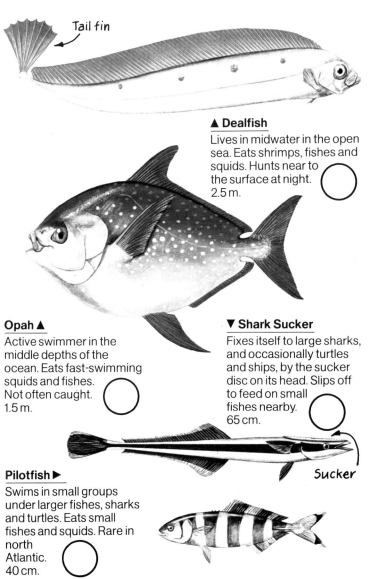

Tail fin

▲ Dealfish
Lives in midwater in the open
sea. Eats shrimps, fishes and
squids. Hunts near to
the surface at night.
2.5 m.

Opah ▲
Active swimmer in the
middle depths of the
ocean. Eats fast-swimming
squids and fishes.
Not often caught.
1.5 m.

▼ Shark Sucker
Fixes itself to large sharks,
and occasionally turtles
and ships, by the sucker
disc on its head. Slips off
to feed on small
fishes nearby.
65 cm.

Sucker

Pilotfish ▶
Swims in small groups
under larger fishes, sharks
and turtles. Eats small
fishes and squids. Rare in
north
Atlantic.
40 cm.

Ocean surface fishes

▲ Bluefish
Very active predator.
Forms schools and attacks
smaller fishes. Occasionally
found in coastal water.
Only in Mediterranean
and south
Atlantic.
70 cm.

▼ Dolphinfish
Fast-swimming migratory
fish which hunts at the
surface. Forehead
becomes steeper with age.
Not in north
Atlantic.
1.9 m.

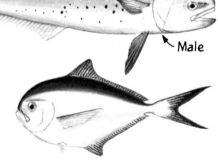

← Male

Ray's Bream ▶
In deep water to south,
but migrates northwards
and is often stranded on
northern coasts. Feeds on
crustaceans
and fishes.
55 cm.

◀ Scabbardfish
Found in water 100-400 m
deep over sandy bottoms.
Eats mainly fishes.
Caught on deep lines and
in trawls. Not
in north
Atlantic. 2 m.

Ocean surface fishes

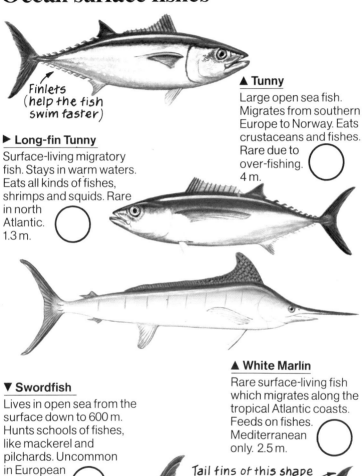

Finlets
(help the fish
swim faster)

▲ Tunny
Large open sea fish.
Migrates from southern
Europe to Norway. Eats
crustaceans and fishes.
Rare due to
over-fishing.
4 m.

▶ Long-fin Tunny
Surface-living migratory
fish. Stays in warm waters.
Eats all kinds of fishes,
shrimps and squids. Rare
in north
Atlantic.
1.3 m.

▲ White Marlin
Rare surface-living fish
which migrates along the
tropical Atlantic coasts.
Feeds on fishes.
Mediterranean
only. 2.5 m.

▼ Swordfish
Lives in open sea from the
surface down to 600 m.
Hunts schools of fishes,
like mackerel and
pilchards. Uncommon
in European
seas.
4.9 m.

Tail fins of this shape
are typical of fast
swimmers

Ocean surface fishes

Sunfish ▼

Open sea fish which feeds on jellyfishes. Lives near the surface of the sea. Its skeleton is light and paper-thin. 4 m.

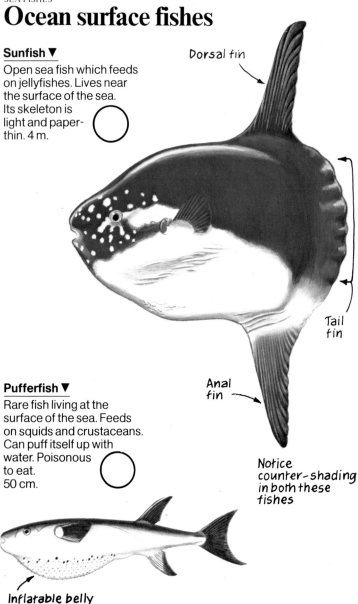

Dorsal fin

Tail fin

Anal fin

Notice counter-shading in both these fishes

Pufferfish ▼

Rare fish living at the surface of the sea. Feeds on squids and crustaceans. Can puff itself up with water. Poisonous to eat. 50 cm.

Inflatable belly

Chapter 5
THE SEASHORE

Introduction to Chapter 5

Chapter Five is an identification guide to the many animals and plants that can be found on the seashore. The species on the following pages are divided into the scientific groups to which they belong and include flowers, corals, molluscs, crustaceans and sponges. Some of the species are very rare in Britain or are not present at all, but are common in other European countries.

The description next to each illustration gives the important features to look for when identifying a species. In most cases the English name is given but for those species which do not have a common English name, the names are in Latin.

Beachcombing

Many of the animals that live on the seashore protect themselves by hiding in rock crevices, among seaweed and under stones and in shady parts of rock pools. These places are worthwhile investigating but remember not to disturb the animals and to carefully replace anything you pick up or move.

Empty shells, crab shells, fishes' egg cases, cuttlebones and pieces of dead seaweed make good souvenirs. Put seaweed in water to see its shape properly. Look for glass rubbed smooth by the sea and for interesting pieces of driftwood, pebbles, corks and fishing nets. *Never* collect living plants and animals.

Tides

The tides are caused by the positions of the Moon and Sun in relation to the Earth. The sea comes up and goes down the beach twice every day, so there are two high tides and two low tides. About every two weeks it comes up higher and goes down lower than usual. These tides are called **spring tides** (nothing to do with the season). Small tides, called **neap tides,** occur in the weeks between the spring tides. Between neap and spring tides, the tides steadily increase and decrease. (The Mediterranean Sea only ever has a very small tide.)

Before you go out, find out from the local paper when the tides are.

Zones

The area between the low water lines of spring and neap tides is called the **lower shore,** and the area between the high water lines of spring and neap tides is called the **upper shore.** The main part of the beach, between these two shores, is called the **middle shore.** If you know when the spring tides are, you can explore the lower shore. The descriptions in this chapter refer to these three areas, so you will find it useful to know them when you go out.

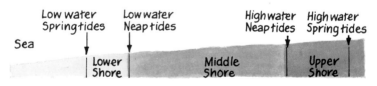

Seashore habitats

There are four main kinds of beach: rocky, sandy, muddy and shingle. The kind of seashore life you find will vary from one to another, although some species live on all kinds of beach. The descriptions tell you on which kind of shore each species lives.

Many of the species live on the shore or in shallow water. Others, like the jellyfishes, live in the sea but can be spotted washed up on the beach. A few, such as dolphins, (see Chapter Seven, page 332), swim close enough to be spotted from the shore. Look on cliffs for birds and plants, and in rock pools for sea anemones and fishes. (See Chapter One for seashore birds and Chapter Four for shallow water fishes.) You can also find seashore life, particularly birds and plants, on saltmarshes and estuaries.

Sandy and muddy shores
Sandy and muddy shores are good places to look for molluscs and worms that live buried beneath the surface. Many plants grow on sand dunes high up on the shore. Look for gulls and wading birds and for fishes in the shallow water.

Rocky shores
Rocky shores are ideal habitats for many plants and animals. Shells hide in crevices, seaweeds cling to the rock surface, and crabs hunt for food in the pools. Look for flowers along cliff tops.

Shingle shores
Little can grow on a shingle beach, because the pebbles are always being moved by the sea and do not hold water when the tide is out. Look for seaweeds and empty shells washed ashore and for barnacles and mussels attached to breakwaters.

Measuring plants and animals

The illustrations of the plants and animals in this chapter are not drawn to scale but their sizes are given in the descriptions. The diagram below shows how they are measured. Take a tape measure with you to help you identify species. Remember that young species will be smaller than the average fully-grown ones.

Flowers	Seaweeds	Sponges	Corals
Sea Anemones	Worms	Octopus	Squids
Shells (univalve)	Shells (bivalve)	Starfish, Brittle Stars	Sea Urchins
Barnacles	Prawns, Shrimps, Lobsters	Crabs	Jellyfish

Other equipment

Apart from a tape measure, you will find some of the following articles useful when you are beach-combing: a magnifying glass for examining small animals and plants, a shrimping net for exploring rock pools and plastic bags for collections of pebbles, seaweed, etc.

Marks in the sand

A sandy beach may look empty, but look closely for signs like these left by seashore animals. Their tracks show up best in wet sand.

Look for the pointed claws of gulls' tracks. The webbing shows only in soft, wet sand.

The Sand Mason lives in the sand in a tube of shell bits. The top of the tube and fringed tip of the worm stick up out of the sand.

The Sea Potato leaves a dent in the sand where it burrows.

A tern's tracks are small, with very narrow webbing.

Sand casts and hollows show at the openings of a Lugworm's burrow.

199

Flowers

Look for flowers on shingle and sandy beaches, cliffs, dunes and saltmarshes.

Pod

Yellow Horned Poppy ▶

Called Horned because of the long green pods, which appear in summer. Flowers June-Sept.
Shingle beaches.
Up to 1 m tall. ◯

Leaf

Flower head

◀ Sea Kale

Grows in clumps on shingle. Broad, fleshy leaves have crinkly edges. Flowers June-August. Up to 1 m tall. ◯

Golden Samphire ▶

Stout plant with shiny, fleshy leaves. Often grows in large clumps on saltmarshes, shingle and cliffs. Flowers in autumn.
60 cm tall. ◯

◀ Sea Sandwort

Also called Sea Purslane. Common creeping plant on loose sand and shingle. Helps to stop sand drifting. Flowers May-August.
30 cm tall. ◯

Flowers

Annual Seablite ▶

Grows along the ground or upright. Clusters of tiny green flowers appear at base of upper leaves July-October. Saltmarshes. 20 cm tall.

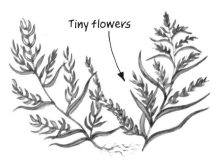

Tiny flowers

Downy leaves

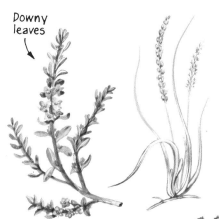

◀ Sea Milkwort (left)

Creeping plant that spreads over grassy saltmarshes. Flowers June-August.

◀ Sea Arrow-Grass (right)

Tough plant with flat sharp leaves. Flowers May-Sept. Grassy saltmarshes. 15-50 cm tall.

Sea Lavender (left) ▶

Tough, woody plant with leaves in a clump near the ground. On muddy saltmarshes. Flowers July-Sept. Up to 40 cm tall.

Sea Aster (right) ▶

Flowers in late summer, with mauve or white petals. Saltmarshes. Up to 1 m tall.

Seaweeds

Gut Laver (left) ▶

Tube-like fronds do not branch. May cover pools on upper shore and in estuaries. Very common. 20 cm.

Sea Lettuce (right) ▶

Common on rocky shores at middle and lower levels. Fronds become dark green with age. 20 cm.

Frond

Disc

◀ Mermaid's Cup

Disc shape on thin stalk made up of many tiny segments pressed close together. On rocks in sheltered bays. Mediterranean. 4-6 cm tall.

Bryopsis (left) ▶

Looks shiny. Found on steep sides of rock pools on middle and lower shore. 7.5 cm.

Sea Chain (right) ▶

Feels hard and brittle because it is covered with lime. Shallow water in sheltered bays. Mediterranean. 15 cm.

Female plant is darker green

Many seaweeds live on the shore, especially on rocky shores. Some can live in and out of the water as the tide comes in and goes out.

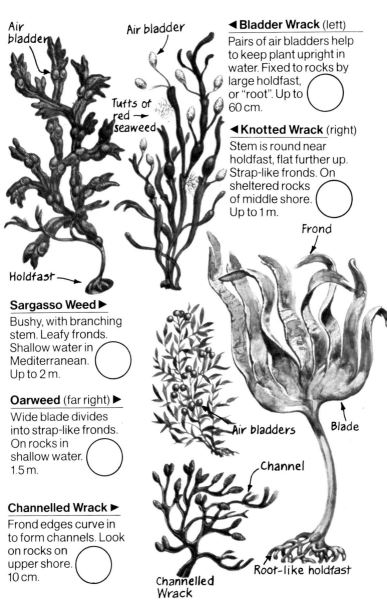

Air bladder

Air bladder

Tufts of red seaweed

Holdfast

◄ Bladder Wrack (left)
Pairs of air bladders help to keep plant upright in water. Fixed to rocks by large holdfast, or "root". Up to 60 cm.

◄ Knotted Wrack (right)
Stem is round near holdfast, flat further up. Strap-like fronds. On sheltered rocks of middle shore. Up to 1 m.

Frond

Sargasso Weed ►
Bushy, with branching stem. Leafy fronds. Shallow water in Mediterranean. Up to 2 m.

Oarweed (far right) **►**
Wide blade divides into strap-like fronds. On rocks in shallow water. 1.5 m.

Channelled Wrack ►
Frond edges curve in to form channels. Look on rocks on upper shore. 10 cm.

Air bladders

Blade

Channel

Channelled Wrack

Root-like holdfast

203

Seaweeds

Phymatolithon ▶
Some red seaweeds, like this one, have a hard coating of lime. It forms a crust in patches on rocks and stones on middle and lower shore.

◀ Laver
Bumpy fronds usually attached at one point. On sand-covered stones, middle to lower shore. Rocks on upper shore. 15 cm.

Plocamium ▶
Small tufted plant with finely-divided fronds. Feathery tips only grow on one side of each branch. Shallow water or washed ashore. 15-20 cm.

◀ Irish Moss
Two forms, broad and narrow, found on rocks on middle and lower shore. Look for the small, disc-shaped holdfast. 15 cm.

Narrow form

Broad form

Holdfast

Sea Oak ▶
Fronds shaped like oak leaves, with markings like veins. Grows on lower shore rocks, in pools and on stalks of large brown seaweeds. 20 cm.

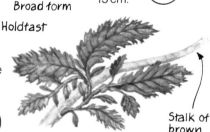

Stalk of brown seaweed

Sponges

Sponges are found mostly low down on the shore, usually on rocks. They look like plants, but are really animals.

◀ Scypha ciliata

Shaggy, upright tube, often with fringed top. Lives singly or in clusters in damp, shady places. On stones or among seaweed. Up to 12 cm long.

Polymastia mamillaris ▶

Can be orange, pink, or yellowy grey. In shallow water, half-buried in muddy gravel. On stones and shells. Up to 8 cm across.

◀ Sea Orange

Round orange sponge. Surface is grooved. Shallow water, but more often seen offshore. Up to 7 cm across.

Haliclona oculata ▶

Looks like a small tree. "Branches" are greyish pink, with openings. Lower shores in fast currents, and estuaries with muddy gravel. Up to 16 cm long.

Regular openings squirt out water

◀ Bread Sponge

Many different shapes, and colour varies from green to yellow. On rocks, shells and seaweed holdfasts. Middle shore and downwards. 10 cm across.

Can be branching shape

Corals

Corals are made up of many tiny animals, called polyps. Their outer skeletons join together to form a large colony.

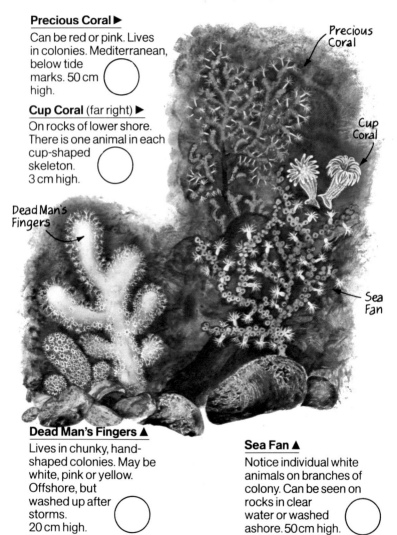

Precious Coral ▶

Can be red or pink. Lives in colonies. Mediterranean, below tide marks. 50 cm high.

Cup Coral (far right) ▶

On rocks of lower shore. There is one animal in each cup-shaped skeleton. 3 cm high.

Precious Coral

Cup Coral

Dead Man's Fingers

Sea Fan

Dead Man's Fingers ▲

Lives in chunky, hand-shaped colonies. May be white, pink or yellow. Offshore, but washed up after storms. 20 cm high.

Sea Fan ▲

Notice individual white animals on branches of colony. Can be seen on rocks in clear water or washed ashore. 50 cm high.

Sea Anemones

These flower-like animals are quite common on rocks, but may be well hidden. When they are not under water their tentacles are drawn in.

Beadlet Anemone ▶

Red or green with a blue spot below each tentacle and a thin blue line round the base.
Common in rock pools. 5 cm high.

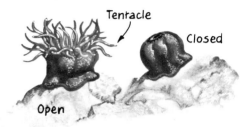

Tentacle

Closed

Open

Feathery tentacles

◀ Plumose Anemone

May be orange or white. Often seen just below water surface on pier supports. 20 cm high.

Snakelocks Anemone ▶

Can be grey or greenish. The sticky tentacles contract when touched, but do not disappear. Rocky shores, sometimes on oarweed. 10 cm across.

◀ Wartlet Anemone

Body varies from green to red, with six rows of white warts and striped tentacles. In lower shore rock pools and crevices. 4 cm across.

Closed

Open

Sea Anemones

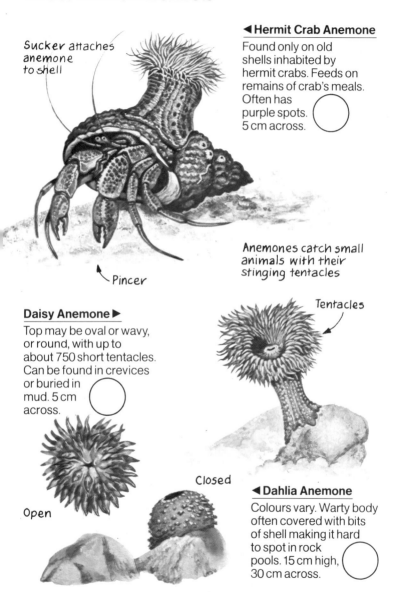

Sucker attaches anemone to shell

Pincer

◀ Hermit Crab Anemone

Found only on old shells inhabited by hermit crabs. Feeds on remains of crab's meals. Often has purple spots. 5 cm across.

Anemones catch small animals with their stinging tentacles

Tentacles

Daisy Anemone ▶

Top may be oval or wavy, or round, with up to about 750 short tentacles. Can be found in crevices or buried in mud. 5 cm across.

Open

Closed

◀ Dahlia Anemone

Colours vary. Warty body often covered with bits of shell making it hard to spot in rock pools. 15 cm high, 30 cm across.

Molluscs

These animals have a hard shell on the outside which protects their soft bodies. Some molluscs live on the seashore. Others live in the sea, but you may find their empty shells washed ashore. Single shells are called univalves. Molluscs that have two shells joined together by muscles, such as cockles, are called bivalves. The empty bivalve shells you find on the beach have often been broken in half by the sea.

Foot is
under shell

Slipper Limpet ▶

Often attached to each other in chains, with females at the bottom and males on top.
2.5 cm wide.

Dog Whelk ▶

Common in rock crevices on barnacles. Colour depends on what food it eats.
3 cm high.

◀ Common Limpet

Clings to rock with muscular foot. Feeds on seaweed at night. Common on rocky shores.
7 cm long.

◀ Common Mussel

On rocky shores and in estuaries, attached to rocks by thin threads. People collect mussels to eat.
1-10 cm long.

◀ Common Periwinkle

Look for it close to the sea on all kinds of shores. Feeds on seaweed.
2.5 cm high.

Molluscs

Common Cerith ▶
On stones, or buried in sand or mud. Hermit crabs use empty shells. Mediterranean. 4.5 cm high.

◀ Dove Shell
Found on rocks in shallow water. Colour varies. Look for empty shells on the beach. Mediterranean. 4.5 cm high.

Painted Topshell ▶
On rocks and under stones. Can be yellow or pink, with red stripes. 2.5 cm high.

◀ Netted Dog Whelk
At or below low tide level on rocky shores. Likes sandy crevices. 2.5 cm high.

Saddle Oyster ▶
Sticks firmly to rocks. Shell often follows shape of rock. Middle shore and below. 6 cm wide.

Mother of pearl ↘

◀ Fool's Cap
Usually in deep water, but may be attached to other shells or rocks low down on the shore. 1.2 cm wide.

Molluscs

Nun Cowrie ▶
Look under stones and in crevices in rocks.
1 cm long.

Dark spots on top of shell

◀ File Shell
White shell with scaly ribs. In rocks crevices and under stones. Mediterranean.
5 cm long.

Ribs →

White Piddock ▶
Burrows into soft rock, wood and firm sand. Found on lower shore.
15 cm long.

◀ Common Oyster
Shell shape varies and two halves are not the same. In shallow and deep water.
10 cm long.

Sting Winkle ▶
Drills a hole in oyster shells to eat the flesh inside.
6 cm high.

◀ Common Whelk
Very common on rocky and sandy beaches. Lower shore.
8 cm high.

Molluscs

Great Topshell ▶
Usually lives in water about 10 m deep, but empty shells are often washed up on shore. Notice reddish zig-zag stripes.
2 cm high.

◀ Variegated Scallop
Can be many different colours. One "ear" is twice as long as the other. Very low down on shore.
6 cm long.

Ear

Lurid Cowrie ▶
On muddy and sandy bottoms, often in very deep water. May be washed ashore in the Mediterranean.
5 cm long.

◀ Dog Cockle
Large thick shell with brown markings. Burrows just below the surface of sand.
6.5 cm long.

Heart Cockle ▶
Look at shell from its side to see heart shape. Lives in muddy sand below low tide level, but may be washed ashore.
9.5 cm wide.

Molluscs

◀ Necklace Shell

Preys on other molluscs. Bores a neat hole in shells and eats flesh inside. On sandy shores. 3 cm high.

Wing Oyster ▶

Named after its shape. Attached to stones in deeper waters of the Mediterranean and Atlantic. Uncommon. 7 cm long.

◀ Common Wentletrap

Look for raised ribs. Usually in deep water, sometimes on rocks on shore. Up to 4 cm high.

Pilgrim's Scallop ▶

One of the largest Mediterranean bivalves. Swims by clapping valves together. Used for making spoons and cups. 13 cm wide.

◀ Mediterranean Tun

Eats other molluscs. Deep water or washed up on shore. 25 cm high.

Molluscs

Razor Shell ▶
Looks like an old-fashioned razor. Lives buried in sand or mud, often 1m down. 15 cm long.

◀ Smooth Venus
Pretty, shiny shell. Lives buried in sand or mud on all Mediterranean and some British shores. 11 cm long.

Baltic Tellin ▶
Eaten by many fish, especially by halibut. Burrows in mud and sand of sea, and salty water of estuaries. 2 cm long.

◀ Elephant's Tusk
Named for its shape. Lives in muddy sand of deeper water of Atlantic Ocean, English Channel and North Sea. 5 cm long.

Trough Shell ▶
People catch them for food. Likes to burrow in clean sand or gravel of lower shores. Widespread. 5 cm long.

Molluscs

◀ Edible Cockle
Very common. Burrows in sand or mud from the lower shore down. Often dug up for food.
5 cm wide.

Screw Shell ▶
Long thin shell often found in large numbers on sandy bottoms in deep water. Empty shells are sometimes washed ashore.
6 cm high.

Band markings

◀ Banded Wedge Shell
Named after band markings. Burrows in the sand on the shore and in water up to 10 m deep. Empty shells often found on the beach.
3.5 cm long.

Pelican's Foot ▶
Its unusual shape makes this shell easy to spot. Large numbers live together on all kinds of seabed.
5.5 cm high.

◀ Common Sand Gaper
So called because two halves of the shell gape when closed. Lives in sand and burrows deeper as it grows. larger.
12 cm wide.

215

Molluscs

Chink Shell ▶
Usually in shallow water,
on seaweeds.
Striped.
1 cm high.

◀ Blue-rayed Limpet
Rows of blue spots are
bright on young shells,
faded on old ones. On
brown seaweeds
and holdfasts.
1.5 cm long.

Mediterranean Cone ▶
Do not touch. Has tooth
filled with poison to
catch prey.
Mediterranean.
Up to 5 cm high.

◀ Horse Mussel
Usually on oarweed from
lower shore to very deep
water. One of Europe's
largest
mussels.
Up to 20 cm long.

Flat Periwinkle ▶
Colours vary. Feeds on wrack
seaweeds. In rock
pools. Common.
1 cm high.

◀ Pheasant Shell
Found mostly on red
seaweeds in rock pools of
lower shore.
The shell is
glossy.
8 mm high.

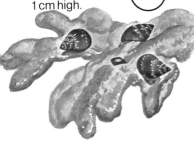

216

Sea Urchins and Brittle Star

These animals have spiny skins, and rows of suckers which they use for pulling themselves along and for holding on to rocks.

Brown Serpent-star ▶

Stripes on arms darken with age.
Mediterranean.
10-15 cm across.

◀ Small Purple-tipped Sea Urchin

Under rocks and stones on lower shore. Atlantic coasts. Spines have purple tips.
Up to 4 cm across.

Test

Edible Sea Urchin ▶

On rocky shores in west Britain, but becoming rare. Spines drop off when sea urchins die. Shell is called a test.
Up to 15 cm across.

Live Sea Urchin

◀ Common Mediterranean Sea Urchin (left)

Holds bits of seaweed or shell over itself.
Not in Britain.
Up to 10 cm across.

◀ Black Sea Urchin (right)

Black spines. Lower shore and deep water.
Not in Britain.
6-10 cm across.

Sea Potato ▶

Sea urchin that lives in sand at lowest tide level. Leaves a dent on surface where it has burrowed. Empty tests may be washed ashore in storms.
5-6 cm long.

Test

Starfishes and Brittle Stars

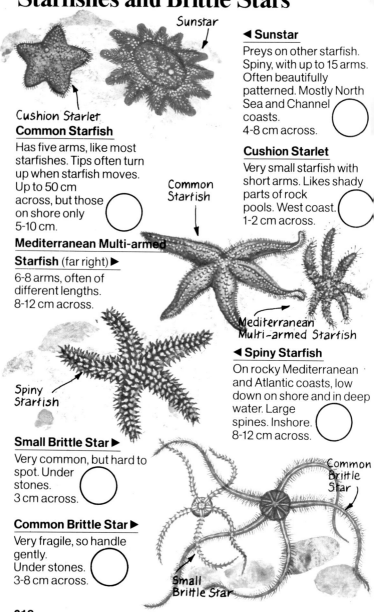

Sunstar

Cushion Starlet

Common Starfish

◀ Sunstar

Preys on other starfish. Spiny, with up to 15 arms. Often beautifully patterned. Mostly North Sea and Channel coasts. 4-8 cm across.

Common Starfish

Has five arms, like most starfishes. Tips often turn up when starfish moves. Up to 50 cm across, but those on shore only 5-10 cm.

Cushion Starlet

Very small starfish with short arms. Likes shady parts of rock pools. West coast. 1-2 cm across.

Mediterranean Multi-armed

Starfish (far right) ▶

6-8 arms, often of different lengths. 8-12 cm across.

Common Starfish

Mediterranean Multi-armed Starfish

Spiny Starfish

◀ Spiny Starfish

On rocky Mediterranean and Atlantic coasts, low down on shore and in deep water. Large spines. Inshore. 8-12 cm across.

Small Brittle Star ▶

Very common, but hard to spot. Under stones. 3 cm across.

Common Brittle Star ▶

Very fragile, so handle gently. Under stones. 3-8 cm across.

Common Brittle Star

Small Brittle Star

Crustaceans

A large group of animals that have shells which protect them.

◀ Acorn Barnacle

Very common on rocks. Often has one broad plate. Its opening is diamond-shaped.
1.5 cm long.

Opening

Plate

Opening

Star Barnacle ▶

Look on rocks. In the south it may be found near Acorn Barnacle, but higher up the beach. The opening is kite-shaped.
1.2 cm long.

◀ Beach Hopper

Jumps about when disturbed. Lives under stones and among seaweed high up on beach. Male has claws on second pair of legs. 2 cm long.

Claw

Sea Scud ▶

Lives on muddy sand and in sheltered estuaries. Hides under stones on middle and lower shore.
1.3 cm long.

◀ Gribble

Lives in wood. Look for the tiny holes it bores into piers and in the hulls of boats.
4 mm long.

Crustaceans

Sea Slater ▶

Look in cracks in
breakwaters and on rocks
above high tide level.
Moves down shore to feed
as tide goes out.
Runs fast.
2.5 cm long.

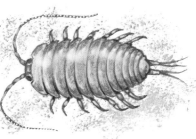

◀ Chameleon Prawn

Usually lives in deep
water, but may be found
among seaweed in lower
shore rock pools. Changes
colour to match
seaweed.
2.5 cm long.

White Shrimp ▶

Common in rock pools on
lower shore and in
shallow water
in sandy
estuaries.
5 cm long.

◀ Common Prawn

Common in shallow water,
sometimes found in rock
pools. Like all prawns and
shrimps, its feelers are
longer than
its body.
6.5 cm long.

Claw

Sand Shrimp ▶

Common in sandy
estuaries. Broad flattened
claws on first legs. People
catch them
to eat.
5 cm long.

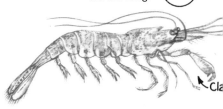

Cla

Crustaceans

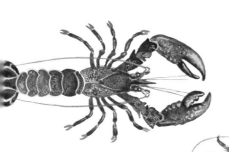

◄ Common Lobster

Small ones sometimes found in lower shore rock pools. It is illegal to take any less than 8 cm long. Strong pincers on front legs are slightly unequal. Up to 45 cm long.

Montagu's Plated Lobster ►

Its last pair of legs are hidden under its body. Found under seaweed and stones. 4 cm long.

◄ Broad-clawed

Porcelain Crab

Notice broad, hairy claws and very small back legs. Under stones. Middle and lower shores. 1.2 cm long.

Long-clawed

Porcelain Crab ►

Long claws are not hairy. Can be found among stones and on oarweed holdfasts on lower shore. 1.2 cm long.

Shell of Common Whelk

◄ Common Hermit Crab

Has no hard shell of its own to protect soft body so lives in empty shell like this one. In rock pools. Up to 10 cm long.

Crustaceans

Sponge Crab ▶

Covered in hairs and looks furry. Often carries piece of sponge on its back, held by last two pairs of legs.
In rock pools.
Rare. 7 cm long.

Antennae

Pincer

◀ Shore Crab

Has smooth, broad shell. Young ones often have attractive markings. Common on sandy and rocky shores.
4 cm long.

Velvet Swimming Crab ▶

Lower shore and shallow water. Red eyes, with 8-10 small points in between, on shell edge.
Hairy shell.
8 cm long.

Broad back legs act as swimming paddles

◀ Pennant's Crab

Has long, smooth shell, and swimming paddles on last pair of legs. Swims near sandy bottom in shallow water.
Burrows fast
3.5 cm long.

Hairy Crab ▶

Has wide, hairy body and large, unequal pincers. Common in some places, and found among stones and seaweed.
Lower shore.
2 cm long.

Crustaceans

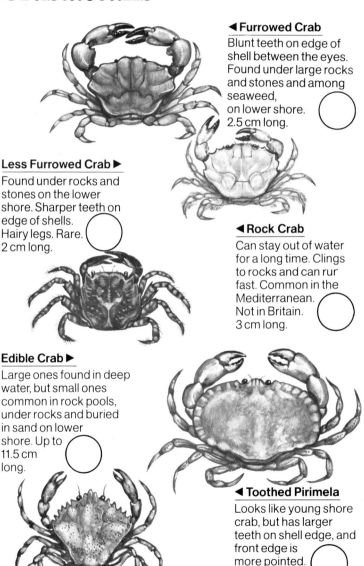

◀ Furrowed Crab
Blunt teeth on edge of shell between the eyes. Found under large rocks and stones and among seaweed, on lower shore. 2.5 cm long.

Less Furrowed Crab ▶
Found under rocks and stones on the lower shore. Sharper teeth on edge of shells. Hairy legs. Rare. 2 cm long.

◀ Rock Crab
Can stay out of water for a long time. Clings to rocks and can run fast. Common in the Mediterranean. Not in Britain. 3 cm long.

Edible Crab ▶
Large ones found in deep water, but small ones common in rock pools, under rocks and buried in sand on lower shore. Up to 11.5 cm long.

◀ Toothed Pirimela
Looks like young shore crab, but has larger teeth on shell edge, and front edge is more pointed. 1 cm long.

Crustaceans

Thornback Spider Crab ▶

Shell is oval and spiny. Often caught in lobster pots. Sometimes in rock pools on lower shore, and in oarweed. 15 cm long.

Beak

◀ Slender-legged
Spider Crab

Notice long beak. Often has bits of seaweed or sponge on shell. Moves slowly. Rock pools. 1.8 cm long.

Toad Crab ▶

Pear-shaped shell often covered with sponges and seaweed. Eyes can be withdrawn into sockets. Lower shore rock pools. 10 cm long.

Common Mussel

◀ Pea Crab

Lives inside bivalve shells. Female is large and soft; male small with hard shell. Up to 1.2 cm long.

Jellyfishes

These animals are not all real jellyfishes, but are closely related. Most live in the sea, but you may see them washed ashore on the beach.

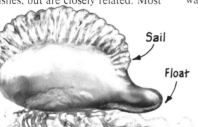

Sail

Float

Tentacles up
up to 20m long

◄ Portuguese Man-o'-War

Really a colony of many tiny individuals living together. Floats on the sea, but sometimes washed ashore. Do not touch: the tentacles can give painful stings. Float 15 cm long.

By-the-Wind Sailor ►

May be blown ashore in winds. Sometimes in shoals. Harmless. Float 3 cm across.

Purple crescents

Four tentacles hang underneath

◄ Moon Jellyfish

Very common on all coasts of Europe and in all oceans of the world. Harmless. Transparent with purple rim and crescents. Up to 15 cm across.

Aequorea ►

Lives in open sea, but often washed up on the beach. Common in late summer. Harmless. Up to 15 cm across.

Jellyfishes

Lion's Mane Jellyfish ▶

This honey-coloured kind is harmless, but a related blue kind stings badly. Both found in Europe, particularly the north. Up to 2 m across.

Lobed edge

Stalked Jellyfish ▼

Does not swim. Body has eight tufts of tentacles round rim. On seaweeds on shore. Harmless. Body is 5 mm high.

Pelagia ▲

Body is mushroom-shaped and has warty surface. Thick tentacles can give painful stings. Lives in open sea, rarely near coast. 10 cm across.

◀ Sea Gooseberry

Transparent body is size and shape of a small gooseberry. Catches prey in two long tentacles. Swims well. Harmless. 1 cm across.

Worms

There are many kinds of worms that live on the shore. Some live in tubes of sand, others burrow in the sand or move on the surface.

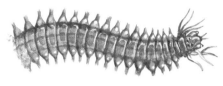

◀ Ragworm

Burrows in sand and mud. Bristles along each side and red line down back. From middle shore to shallow water. 10 cm long.

Gills for breathing

Lugworm ▶

Fat worm with thin tail. Lives buried in sand. Sand casts and hollows show where two ends of its burrow are. 15 cm long.

Worm in tube

◀ Sand Mason

Long thin worm that lives in a tube buried in the sand. Tip of tube, made of sand and shell bits, sticks up above surface. 20 cm long.

Green Leaf Worm ▶

Crawls among barnacles and under seaweed on rocks, or hides in rock crevices. Upper shore to shallow water. 10 cm long.

◀ Keelworm

Worm lives in hard white tube that has a ridge along the top. Look for the tubes on rocks, stones and empty shells. Up to 3 cm long.

Cuttlefish, Octopus, Squids

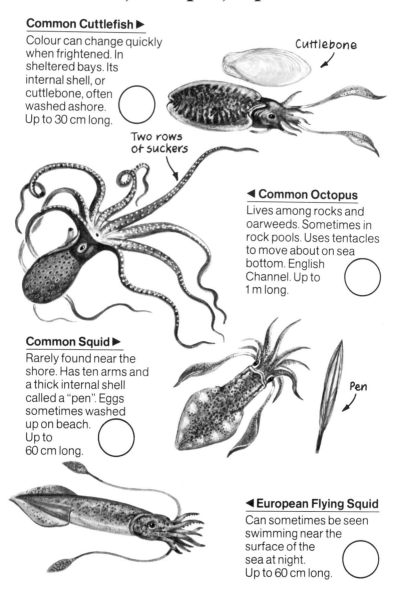

Common Cuttlefish ▶
Colour can change quickly when frightened. In sheltered bays. Its internal shell, or cuttlebone, often washed ashore. Up to 30 cm long.

Cuttlebone

Two rows of suckers

◀ Common Octopus
Lives among rocks and oarweeds. Sometimes in rock pools. Uses tentacles to move about on sea bottom. English Channel. Up to 1 m long.

Common Squid ▶
Rarely found near the shore. Has ten arms and a thick internal shell called a "pen". Eggs sometimes washed up on beach. Up to 60 cm long.

Pen

◀ European Flying Squid
Can sometimes be seen swimming near the surface of the sea at night. Up to 60 cm long.

Chapter 6
INSECTS

Introduction to Chapter 6

This chapter will help you to identify some of the insects of Britain and Europe. There are more than 20,000 different species in Britain alone; only a selection of common ones and a few rarer ones are included here.

Insects are divided scientifically into orders (butterflies and beetles are separate orders) and insects from all the main orders are described. The males and females of some species differ from each other and in these cases both males and females are usually shown. The symbol ♀ means female and ♂ means male. If the larva (caterpillar or nymph) is more commonly seen than the adult insect or is of particular interest it is also shown.

The description next to each insect gives important features to look for and its habitat. If the description says an insect lives in

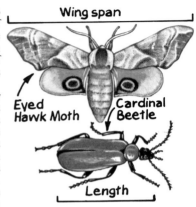

the south, it means the south of Britain. The insect's *approximate* adult length (excluding antennae) or the wing span (W.S.) is also given. If the insect has been enlarged, the line next to the illustration shows its actual size. All the other insects are drawn life size or a little smaller.

The structure of insects

Insects have six legs and their bodies are made up of three distinct parts – head, thorax and abdomen (although there are exceptions such as silverfish). Many insects have one or two pairs of wings but in some, beetles for example, the wings are covered by hard wing cases making the wings difficult to see. Adult insects have a pair of antennae which they use for feeling and smelling, and two large compound eyes.

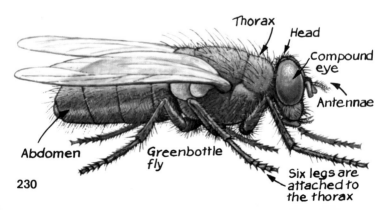

The insect life cycle

All insects lay eggs, but these do not usually hatch into adult insects. Some insects pass through two more stages before becoming adult. The egg hatches into a larva which later becomes a pupa (or chrysalis). This process is called complete metamorphosis. The Seven-spot Ladybird illustrated below is an example.

The female lays her eggs under leaves and on plant stems where there are plenty of aphids for them to feed on when they hatch. The larva grows rapidly, moulting its skin several times before it finally changes into a pupa. The pupa is encased in a hard skin and attached to a leaf or stem by its tail. In about a week the skin of the pupa splits and the fully-grown adult emerges.

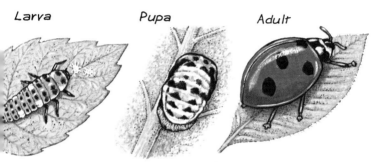

Larva   Pupa   Adult

The eggs of some insects, such as crickets, bugs, and the dragonfly shown below, hatch into larvae called nymphs. Although they have no proper wings at first, nymphs grow into adult insects without changing into pupae. This is called incomplete metamorphosis.

The female dragonfly lays hundreds of eggs; some species drop the eggs into the water where they sink to the bottom, while others lay them in the stems of water plants or on floating weeds. When the nymphs hatch they live either in mud on the water bed or among plants. The nymph lives for about a year and as it grows it moults its skin several times. During the final moult, the skin splits along the back and the adult dragonfly emerges.

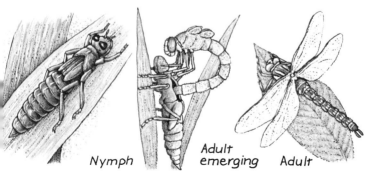

Nymph   Adult emerging   Adult

Butterflies

The butterflies are arranged in order of the families to which they belong. Each one is shown with its wings open and its wings closed, as the markings on the underside are often different from those on the upperside.

Monarch
Also called Milkweed. A rare visitor from America and the largest butterfly found in Britain. Visits bramble, ragwort and other flowers. Open places. W.S. 103-106 mm.

Wall Brown

Often rests on walls and paths. Likes rough, open ground and woodland glades. Flies slowly. Caterpillar eats grasses.
W.S. 44-46 mm.

Caterpillar

Large Wall Brown

Often settles on stony paths in hills and mountains.
Not in Britain.
W.S. 50-56 mm.

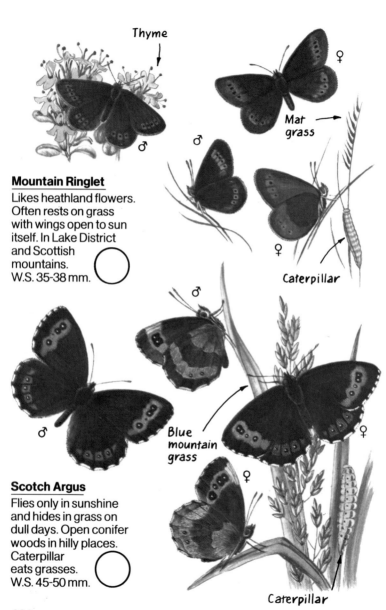

Thyme

♀

Mat grass

♂

Mountain Ringlet

Likes heathland flowers.
Often rests on grass
with wings open to sun
itself. In Lake District
and Scottish
mountains.
W.S. 35-38 mm.

♂

♀

Caterpillar

♂

♂

Blue mountain grass

♀

Scotch Argus

Flies only in sunshine
and hides in grass on
dull days. Open conifer
woods in hilly places.
Caterpillar
eats grasses.
W.S. 45-50 mm.

♀

Caterpillar

234

Orange-brown
European form

♂

♀

Bramble

♂

♀

Speckled Wood

Likes bramble flowers.
Often settles on
sun-spotted leaves in
woods and forests.
Caterpillar
eats grasses.
W.S. 47-50 mm.

Arran Brown

May visit flowers but rests
mostly on grasses. Open
grassland, near woods or
forests. Not
in Britain.
W.S. 48-54 mm.

Grayling

May visit field scabious
and other flowers, but
mostly rests on the
ground with wings closed.
Sandy places and
chalk downs.
W.S. 56-61 mm.

Great Banded Grayling

Likes lucerne and other
flowers, but mostly rests
on the ground with
closed wings. Open
woodland.
Not in Britain.
W.S. 66-72 mm.

Lucerne

Knapweed

♂

♀

♂

♀

Marbled White

Flies in meadows and grassy fields. Likes thistles, knapweed and other roadside flowers. Caterpillar eats grasses. W.S. 53-58 mm.

Large Ringlet

Rests mainly on grasses. In mountains. Caterpillar eats grasses. Not in Britain. W.S. 42-46 mm.

Meadow Brown ▶

Meadows and grassy places where it visits thistles, knapweed and bramble flowers. Active even on dull days. Caterpillar eats grasses. W.S. 50-55 mm.

Bramble

◀ Ringlet

Keeps to damp, grassy places and sunny woodland paths. Visits thistles, knapweed and bramble flowers. W.S. 48-52 mm.

Thistle

Hawkweed

◀ Small Heath

Not fussy about where it lives, and found in open woods, on marshes and on dry hillsides. Likes hawkweed. W.S. 33-35 mm.

♂

♀

♀

♂

Gatekeeper
or Hedge Brown

Basks in sunshine on roadside hedges, especially on bramble. Most common in the south. W.S. 40-46 mm.

Bramble

♀

The colours of this butterfly vary a lot

♂

Heather

♀

♂

Large Heath

Sometimes visits heath flowers, but mostly rests on grasses with wings closed. Likes damp places. Caterpillar eats moorland grasses. W.S. 33-35 mm.

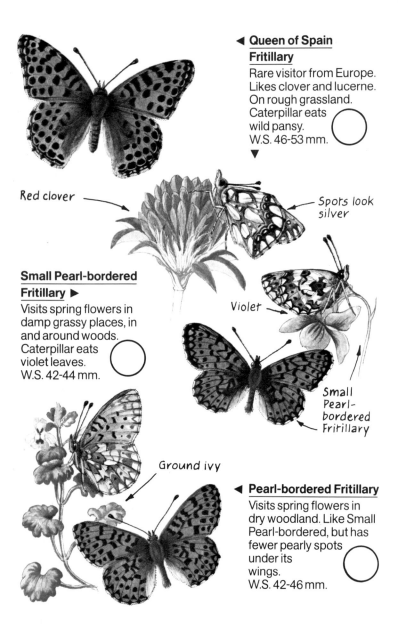

◀ Queen of Spain Fritillary

Rare visitor from Europe. Likes clover and lucerne. On rough grassland. Caterpillar eats wild pansy. W.S. 46-53 mm. ▼

Red clover

Spots look silver

Small Pearl-bordered Fritillary ▶

Visits spring flowers in damp grassy places, in and around woods. Caterpillar eats violet leaves. W.S. 42-44 mm.

Violet

Small Pearl-bordered Fritillary

Ground ivy

◀ Pearl-bordered Fritillary

Visits spring flowers in dry woodland. Like Small Pearl-bordered, but has fewer pearly spots under its wings. W.S. 42-46 mm.

The butterflies on this page
are smaller than life size

Dark Green Fritillary ▶

Likes thistle and bramble
flowers. Open grassland
near woods, and high
rough ground.
Flies fast.
W.S. 63-70 mm.

Thistle

Bracken

Dark
female form

Violet

Silver-washed Fritillary ▶

Likes bramble flowers.
Rests on bracken with
open wings. Woods in
southern England.
Strong flier.
W.S. 72-76 mm.

Bramble

241

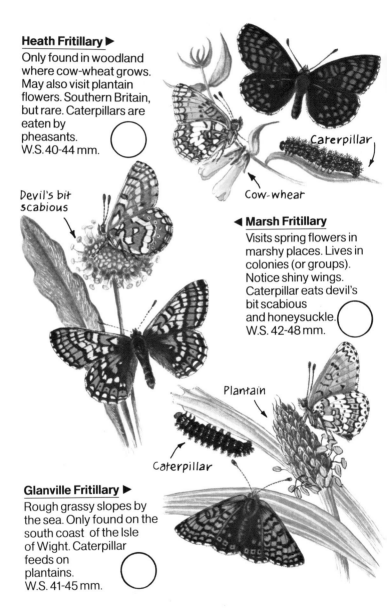

Heath Fritillary ▶

Only found in woodland where cow-wheat grows. May also visit plantain flowers. Southern Britain, but rare. Caterpillars are eaten by pheasants.
W.S. 40-44 mm.

Caterpillar

Cow-wheat

Devil's bit scabious

◀ Marsh Fritillary

Visits spring flowers in marshy places. Lives in colonies (or groups). Notice shiny wings. Caterpillar eats devil's bit scabious and honeysuckle.
W.S. 42-48 mm.

Plantain

Caterpillar

Glanville Fritillary ▶

Rough grassy slopes by the sea. Only found on the south coast of the Isle of Wight. Caterpillar feeds on plantains.
W.S. 41-45 mm.

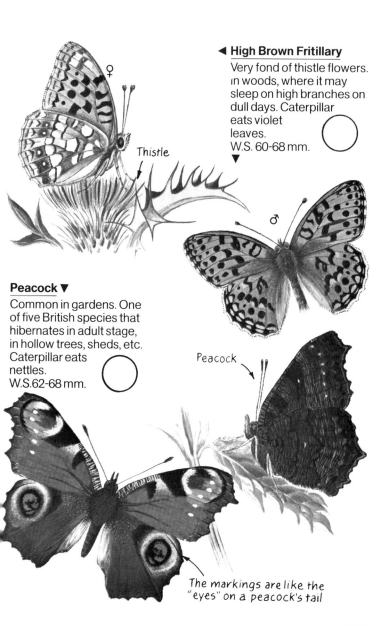

◄ High Brown Fritillary
Very fond of thistle flowers. In woods, where it may sleep on high branches on dull days. Caterpillar eats violet leaves.
W.S. 60-68 mm.
▼

♀

Thistle

♂

Peacock ▼
Common in gardens. One of five British species that hibernates in adult stage, in hollow trees, sheds, etc. Caterpillar eats nettles.
W.S. 62-68 mm.

Peacock

The markings are like the "eyes" on a peacock's tail

◀ Painted Lady

Arrives in spring from
North Africa. Lays eggs on
thistles. Adult insects can
be seen in autumn, but
do not survive
the winter.
W.S. 62-65 mm.

Red Admiral

Painted
Lady

Red Admiral ▶

Common in gardens on
buddleia and Michaelmas
daisies. Migrates here
from North Africa.
Caterpillar feeds
on nettles.
W.S. 66-68 mm.

Thistle

Small
Tortoiseshell

◀ Small Tortoiseshell

Name comes from pattern
on wings. Visits many
flowers and is common all
over Britain. On the wing
from April
to November.
W.S. 48-52 mm.

244

Large Tortoiseshell ▶
Rare. Likes bramble
flowers. Rests on leaves
of tall trees in lanes
and edges of woods.
Caterpillars feed on elm
and goat
willow.
W.S. 62-66 mm.
▼

Nettle

Camberwell
Beauty

◀ Camberwell Beauty
Rare visitor from
Scandinavia, and does not
breed in Britain. Yellow
wing borders turn white
with age. On hills and
visits
gardens.
W.S. 70-73 mm.

Comma

Easy to recognize by its ragged wing edges and the shape of a letter "c" on underside of its wings. In woods and gardens.
W.S. 56-58 mm.

Comma ♂

♀

Comma

Willow

Smaller than life size

When Lesser Purple Emperor's wings catch the light they shimmer purple

Lesser Purple Emperor

Does not visit flowers, but drinks from puddles and may settle on dead animals. In woods. Lays eggs on poplar and willow.
Not in Britain.
W.S. 66-70 mm.

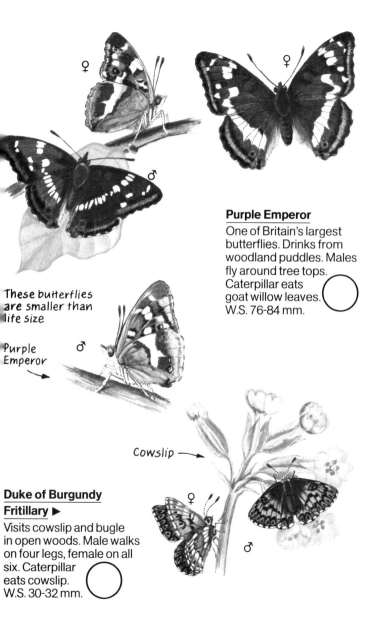

♀

♀

♂

These butterflies
are smaller than
life size

Purple
Emperor

♂

Purple Emperor
One of Britain's largest
butterflies. Drinks from
woodland puddles. Males
fly around tree tops.
Caterpillar eats
goat willow leaves.
W.S. 76-84 mm.

Cowslip →

Duke of Burgundy
Fritillary ▶
Visits cowslip and bugle
in open woods. Male walks
on four legs, female on all
six. Caterpillar
eats cowslip.
W.S. 30-32 mm.

♀

♂

The butterflies on this page are smaller than life size

Strawberry tree

Two-tailed Pasha

Rare. Near Mediterranean and North African coasts. Male very active and flies fast. Caterpillar lives on strawberry tree. W.S. 76-82 mm.

♂

♂

♀

♀

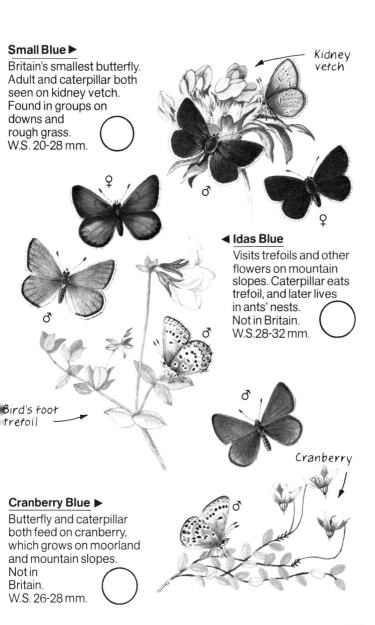

Small Blue ▶

Britain's smallest butterfly.
Adult and caterpillar both
seen on kidney vetch.
Found in groups on
downs and
rough grass.
W.S. 20-28 mm.

Kidney
vetch

♀

♂

♀

♂

◀ Idas Blue

Visits trefoils and other
flowers on mountain
slopes. Caterpillar eats
trefoil, and later lives
in ants' nests.
Not in Britain.
W.S. 28-32 mm.

♂

Bird's foot
trefoil

♂

Cranberry

Cranberry Blue ▶

Butterfly and caterpillar
both feed on cranberry,
which grows on moorland
and mountain slopes.
Not in
Britain.
W.S. 26-28 mm.

♂

Brown Argus

Usually flies on chalk
downs and limestone hills
where rock rose grows.
Visits flowers on warm
sunny days.
Flies fast.
W.S. 28-30 mm.

♂

♂

♀

Common
rock rose →

♀

Caterpillar

Hoary
rock rose →

The markings of this
butterfly vary —
sometimes it has
no white spots

Mountain or Scotch
Brown Argus

Easily recognized by the
white dot on front wing.
Sheltered moorland and
grassy roadsides in
Scotland. Visits
rock rose.
W.S. 28-30 mm.

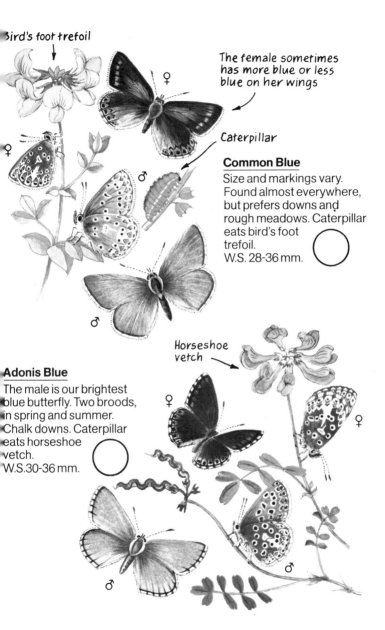

Bird's foot trefoil

♀

The female sometimes has more blue or less blue on her wings

♂

Caterpillar

Common Blue
Size and markings vary. Found almost everywhere, but prefers downs and rough meadows. Caterpillar eats bird's foot trefoil.
W.S. 28-36 mm.

♂

Horseshoe vetch

Adonis Blue
The male is our brightest blue butterfly. Two broods, in spring and summer. Chalk downs. Caterpillar eats horseshoe vetch.
W.S. 30-36 mm.

♀

♀

♂

♂

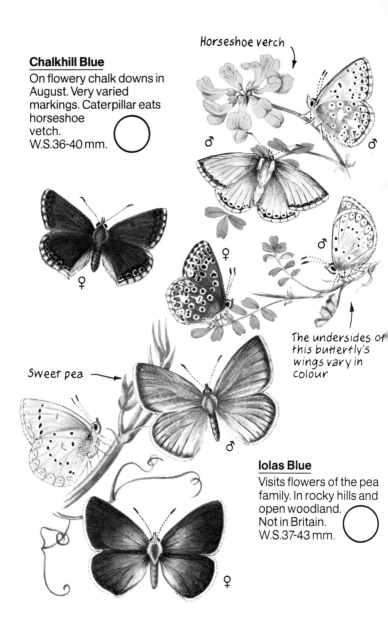

Chalkhill Blue

On flowery chalk downs in
August. Very varied
markings. Caterpillar eats
horseshoe
vetch.
W.S.36-40 mm.

Horseshoe vetch

♂

♂

♀

♂

The undersides of
this butterfly's
wings vary in
colour

Sweet pea

♀

Iolas Blue

Visits flowers of the pea
family. In rocky hills and
open woodland.
Not in Britain.
W.S.37-43 mm.

♀

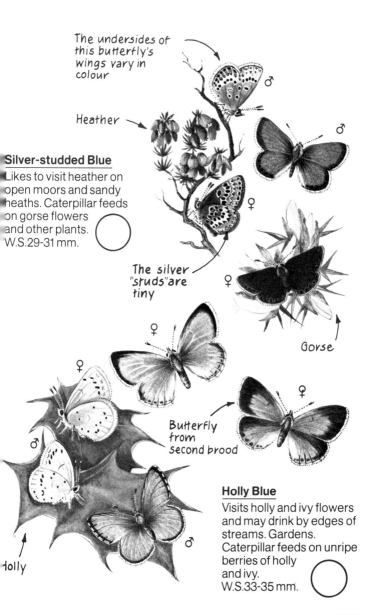

The undersides of this butterfly's wings vary in colour

Heather →

♂

♂

Silver-studded Blue
Likes to visit heather on open moors and sandy heaths. Caterpillar feeds on gorse flowers and other plants. W.S.29-31 mm.

♀

The silver "studs" are tiny

♀

Gorse

♀

♂

♀

Butterfly from second brood

♀

♂

Holly →

Holly Blue
Visits holly and ivy flowers and may drink by edges of streams. Gardens. Caterpillar feeds on unripe berries of holly and ivy. W.S.33-35 mm.

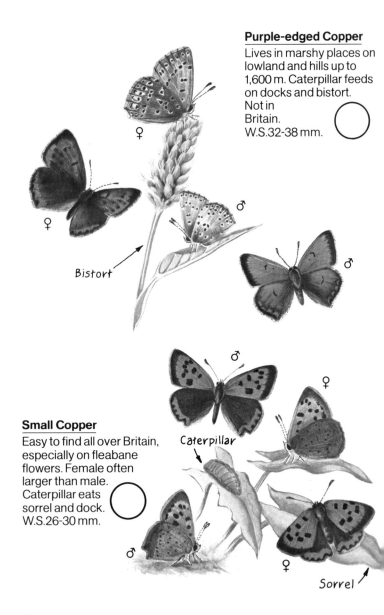

Purple-edged Copper

Lives in marshy places on lowland and hills up to 1,600 m. Caterpillar feeds on docks and bistort. Not in Britain. W.S.32-38 mm.

♀

♀

♂

Bistort

♂

Small Copper

Easy to find all over Britain, especially on fleabane flowers. Female often larger than male. Caterpillar eats sorrel and dock. W.S.26-30 mm.

♂

♀

Caterpillar

♂

♀

Sorrel

Green Hairstreak

Hard to spot because of green underwings which camouflage it on leaves. Quite common on downs, moors, edges of woods, where gorse and broom grow. W.S.31-34mm.

Gorse

♂

♀

♂

♀

♀

♂

Brown Hairstreak

Shy butterfly, not often seen flying. Rests on leaves of blackthorn in August and September. Edges of woods and hedges. W.S.40-42 mm.

♂

Notice the tails

Blackthorn

♀

Oak

Purple Hairstreak

Flies round tree tops in big oak woods. Rests on oak leaves and visits bramble flowers. Caterpillar eats oak leaves.
W.S.36-39 mm.

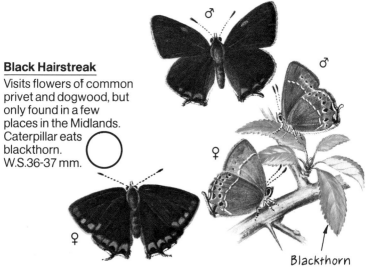

Black Hairstreak

Visits flowers of common privet and dogwood, but only found in a few places in the Midlands. Caterpillar eats blackthorn.
W.S.36-37 mm.

Blackthorn

White Letter Hairstreak

Named after white mark, like a letter "w", on underside of hind wings. Often rests on leaves of wych elm. Open woods and lanes. W.S. 34-35 mm.

Wych elm

♀

Notice the "W"

♂

♀

♂

♀

♂

♂

♀

Blue-spot Hairstreak

Likes rough, hilly places with bushes. Visits privet and other flowers. Caterpillar eats blackthorn. Not in Britain. W.S. 29-33 mm.

The butterflies on this page are smaller than life size

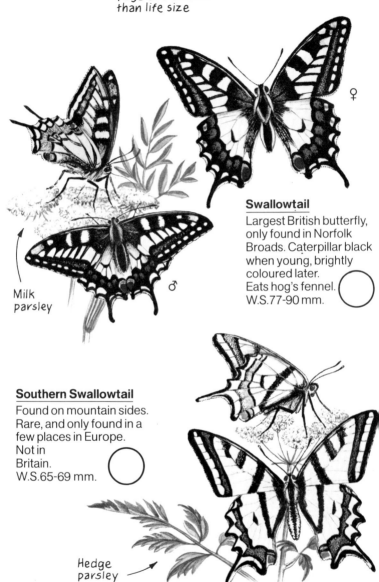

Milk parsley

♀

♂

Swallowtail

Largest British butterfly, only found in Norfolk Broads. Caterpillar black when young, brightly coloured later. Eats hog's fennel. W.S.77-90 mm.

Southern Swallowtail

Found on mountain sides. Rare, and only found in a few places in Europe. Not in Britain. W.S.65-69 mm.

Hedge parsley

The butterflies on this page are smaller than life size

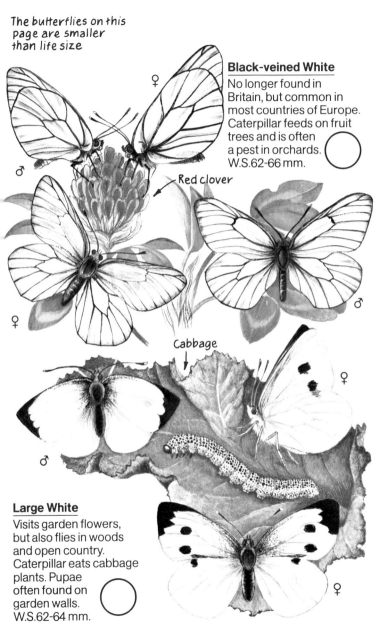

Black-veined White

No longer found in Britain, but common in most countries of Europe. Caterpillar feeds on fruit trees and is often a pest in orchards. W.S.62-66 mm.

Red clover

♀

♂

♂

♀

Cabbage

♀

♂

Large White

Visits garden flowers, but also flies in woods and open country. Caterpillar eats cabbage plants. Pupae often found on garden walls. W.S.62-64 mm.

♀

Small White

Appears in May and August.
Lays single eggs on
cabbages and nasturtiums.
Common in
gardens.
W.S. 48-50 mm.

♂

♀

♂

♀

♂

♀

Green-veined White

Pattern on underwing
helps to protect the
butterfly from enemies
when it sits on grass.
Caterpillar eats leaves
and seed pods of
Jack-by-the-Hedge.
W.S. 47-50 mm.

♀

♂

Wild mignonette

♀

♂

Bath White

Sometimes visits Britain, but rarely in large numbers. Fond of clover and wild mignonette flowers. W.S. 48-52 mm.

♀

♂

♂

♂

♀

Peak White

Only found on grassy slopes high up in mountains. Visits wild mignonette. Not in Britain. W.S. 44-52 mm.

♀

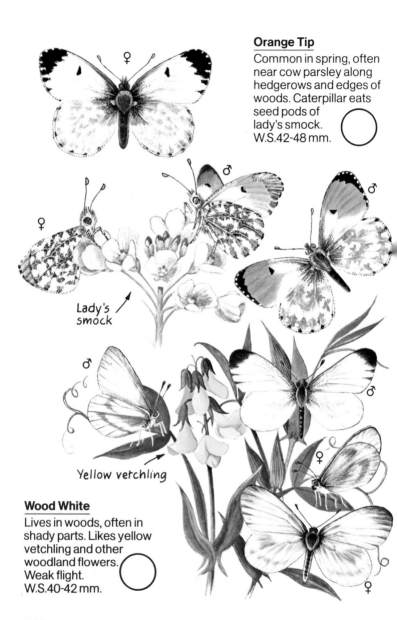

Orange Tip
Common in spring, often near cow parsley along hedgerows and edges of woods. Caterpillar eats seed pods of lady's smock. W.S.42-48 mm.

Lady's smock

Yellow vetchling

Wood White
Lives in woods, often in shady parts. Likes yellow vetchling and other woodland flowers. Weak flight. W.S.40-42 mm.

Pale Clouded Yellow

Rare visitor to Britain from Africa. Likes clover and lucerne. Caterpillar cannot survive through our damp winter. W.S. 52-54 mm.

♀

♂

Zigzag clover

♂

♀

♀

♂

Red clover

Clouded Yellow

Arrives here in spring from Mediterranean. Eggs laid on clover and lucerne. Second brood in autumn, but butterflies do not survive our winter. W.S. 58-62 mm.

♀

The female's colour varies

263

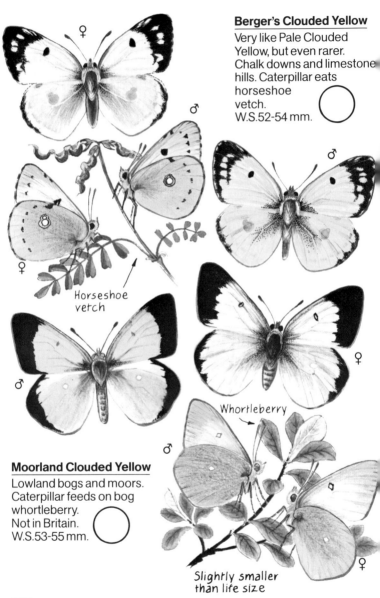

Berger's Clouded Yellow
Very like Pale Clouded Yellow, but even rarer. Chalk downs and limestone hills. Caterpillar eats horseshoe vetch.
W.S. 52-54 mm.

♀

♂

♂

♀

♂

Horseshoe vetch

Whortleberry

♂

Moorland Clouded Yellow
Lowland bogs and moors. Caterpillar feeds on bog whortleberry.
Not in Britain.
W.S. 53-55 mm.

♀

Slightly smaller than life size

The butterflies on this page are slightly smaller than life size

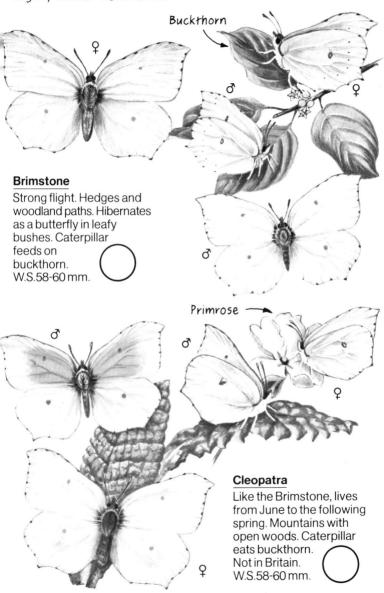

Buckthorn

♀

♂

♀

♂

Brimstone

Strong flight. Hedges and woodland paths. Hibernates as a butterfly in leafy bushes. Caterpillar feeds on buckthorn. W.S.58-60 mm.

Primrose

♂

♂

♀

Cleopatra

Like the Brimstone, lives from June to the following spring. Mountains with open woods. Caterpillar eats buckthorn. Not in Britain. W.S.58-60 mm.

♀

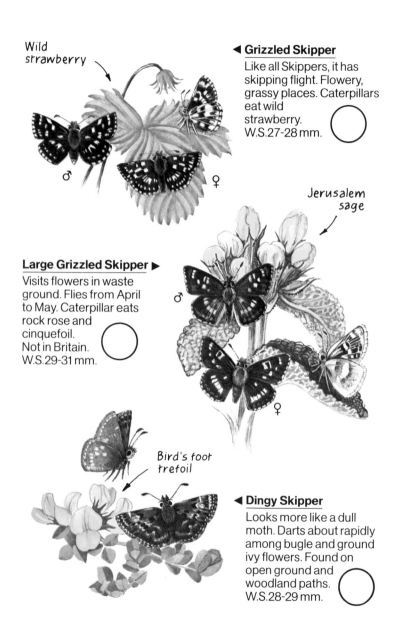

Wild
strawberry

◄ Grizzled Skipper
Like all Skippers, it has
skipping flight. Flowery,
grassy places. Caterpillars
eat wild
strawberry.
W.S.27-28 mm.

♂

♀

Jerusalem
sage

Large Grizzled Skipper ►
Visits flowers in waste
ground. Flies from April
to May. Caterpillar eats
rock rose and
cinquefoil.
Not in Britain.
W.S.29-31 mm.

♂

♀

Bird's foot
trefoil

◄ Dingy Skipper
Looks more like a dull
moth. Darts about rapidly
among bugle and ground
ivy flowers. Found on
open ground and
woodland paths.
W.S.28-29 mm.

Chequered Skipper ▶

Brighter than other
Skippers. Likes bugle, and
suns itself on grasses in
woods. Caterpillar eats
brome grass.
Rare.
W.S.27-29 mm.

Bugle

♀

♂

Bugle

◀ Northern Chequered Skipper

Visits bugle and other
spring flowers in woods
and grassland. Caterpillar
eats grasses.
Not in Britain.
W.S.27-29 mm.

♂

Large Chequered Skipper ▶

Likes damp meadows full
of flowers, and shady
paths in woods. Often
rests on grasses.
Not in Britain.
W.S.32-36 mm.

♀

Wood
false-brome

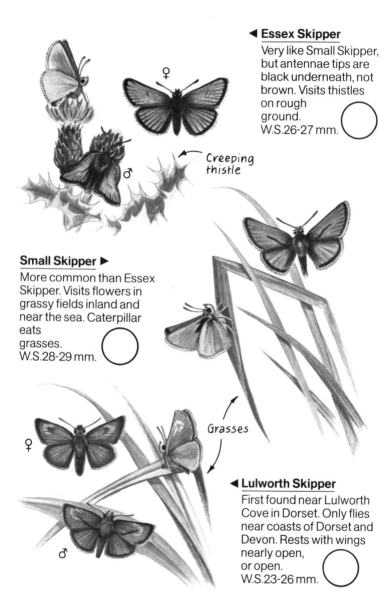

◀ Essex Skipper
Very like Small Skipper, but antennae tips are black underneath, not brown. Visits thistles on rough ground.
W.S.26-27 mm.

Creeping thistle

Small Skipper ▶
More common than Essex Skipper. Visits flowers in grassy fields inland and near the sea. Caterpillar eats grasses.
W.S.28-29 mm.

Grasses

◀ Lulworth Skipper
First found near Lulworth Cove in Dorset. Only flies near coasts of Dorset and Devon. Rests with wings nearly open, or open.
W.S.23-26 mm.

Large Skipper

Commonest Skipper.
Visits bramble and thistle
flowers in grassy lanes
and open woodland.
Flies from June
to August.
W.S. 30-32 mm.

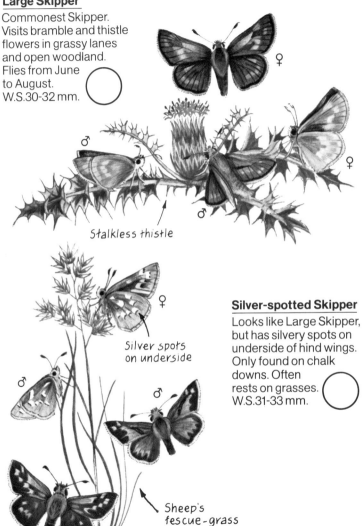

Stalkless thistle

Silver spots
on underside

Silver-spotted Skipper

Looks like Large Skipper,
but has silvery spots on
underside of hind wings.
Only found on chalk
downs. Often
rests on grasses.
W.S. 31-33 mm.

Sheep's
fescue-grass

Moths

Moths belong to the same order as butterflies, but unlike butterflies, which fly during the day, moths are nocturnal. Their antennae are not club-ended like those of butterflies.

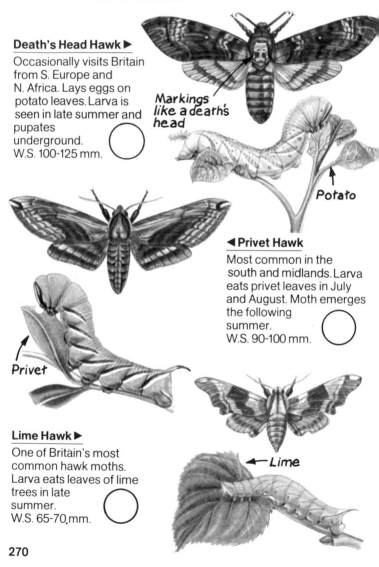

Death's Head Hawk ▶

Occasionally visits Britain from S. Europe and N. Africa. Lays eggs on potato leaves. Larva is seen in late summer and pupates underground. W.S. 100-125 mm.

Markings like a death's head

Potato

◀ Privet Hawk

Most common in the south and midlands. Larva eats privet leaves in July and August. Moth emerges the following summer. W.S. 90-100 mm.

Privet

Lime Hawk ▶

One of Britain's most common hawk moths. Larva eats leaves of lime trees in late summer. W.S. 65-70 mm.

Lime

Moths

Eyed Hawk ▶

Flashes markings on its underwings to frighten birds and other enemies. Larva feeds on sallow and leaves of plum and apple trees. W.S. 75-80 mm.

Eye-like markings

White points

Apple

◀ Poplar Hawk

Common all over Britain. Larva feeds on poplar or sallow and, like Eyed Hawk, has rough skin surface. Notice yellow markings. W.S. 75-80 mm.

Yellow points

Poplar

Hummingbird Hawk ▶

Visitor to Britain. Gardens during day. Hovers over flowers to feed, beating its wings like a hummingbird. Lays eggs on bedstraw. W.S. 45 mm.

Bedstraw

Moths

Elephant Hawk ▶

Widespread, but scarce in Scotland. Larva tapers at head end like an elephant's trunk. It feeds on willowherb and bedstraw.
W.S. 65 mm.

Willowherb

♀

♂

Sloe

◀ Emperor

All over Britain. Male flies by day over moorland, looking for female which comes out at dusk. Lays eggs on heather, bramble, etc. Appearance of larva changes when each skin is shed.
W.S. female 70 mm.
Male 55 mm.

Puss ▶

Widespread in Britain. Lays eggs, usually singly, on willow or sallow in May-June. Thin red "whips" come out of larva's tails, perhaps to frighten birds.
W.S. 65-80 mm.

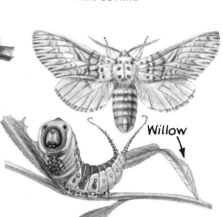

Willow

Moths

Lobster ▶

S. England, Wales and parts of S. Ireland. Name comes from the shape of the larva's tail end. Larva eats beech. W.S. 65-70 mm.

Hind end of larva looks like lobster's claw

Beech

Hawthorn

♂

♀

◀ Vapourer

Common all over Britain, even in towns. Female has only wing stubs and cannot fly. Larva feeds on a variety of trees. W.S. 35 mm.

Peach blossom pattern

Peach Blossom ▶

Found in woodland. Name comes from pattern on wings. Often attracted by "sugaring" Larva feeds on bramble. W.S. 35 mm.

Bramble

Moths

Hawthorn

◀ Yellow-tail
Brightly coloured larvae
are often found in
hedgerows of hawthorn,
sloe and bramble
in May and June.
W.S. 32-40 mm.

Merveille-du-Jour

Oak

Merveille-du-Jour ▶
Oak woodlands. Forewings
match background of tree
bark making moth difficult
for enemies to see.
Larva eats
oak leaves.
W.S. 45 mm.

Alder
Moth

Alder

◀ Alder
Like many other species,
the larva is more striking
than the adult moth. It
feeds on a variety of trees,
including alder
and oak.
W.S. 37 mm.

Moths

Clifden Nonpareil or
Blue Underwing ▶

Breeds in a few places in
Kent, but sometimes visits
other parts of Britain,
usually in late summer.
Stick-like larva feeds on
black poplar
and aspen.
W.S. 90 mm.

Colour of upper
wings matches
tree bark

◀ Red Underwing

Quite common in south
and midlands. Flashes
underwings when
threatened by birds. Rests
in daytime on trees. Larva
eats poplar
and willow.
W.S. 80 mm.

Larva of Red
Underwing

Willow

Face-like
markings
on wings

Mother Shipton ▶

Flies on bright sunny days.
Look on railway banks and
in meadows in May and
June. Larva eats vetches
and clover. Mother Shipton
was a seer who
lived from
1488-1561.
W.S. 35 mm.

Clover

Larva of
Mother Shipton

275

Moths

Y-shaped marking

◄ Silver Y

Visitor to Britain, some years in great numbers. Feeds on garden flowers with long proboscis. Flies fast. Larva eats nettle, thistle, etc. W.S. 40 mm.

Herald ►

Widespread in Britain. Hibernates during the winter in barns, sometimes in small groups. Mates in spring and female lays eggs on various kinds of willow. W.S. 40 mm.

Larva of Herald

Willow

This is Northern Eggar, more common in north of England and Scotland

Female is larger and paler ♂

◄ Oak Eggar

Male flies by day searching for female who rests in heather on moorland. Larva eats heather, bramble, hawthorn, etc. W.S. 50-65 mm.

Hawthorn

Moths

Lappet ►

Name comes from "lappets" on larva. Feeds on apple, sallow and hawthorn. Adult's brown colour, ragged wing edges and veined wings make it look like a bunch of leaves. W.S. 60-70 mm.

← Projection or lappet

Sallow

Wing pattern varies

◄ Wood Tiger

Smaller and more local than Garden Tiger. Widespread on hillsides, heaths and open woodland. Larva eats violets and forget-me-nots, and hibernates. W.S. 35-40 mm.

Plantain

Garden Tiger ►

Common, but larva more often seen. Feeds on many low-growing plants and hibernates when young. Feeds again in spring and is fully grown by June. W.S. 60-70 mm.

Larva is called "woolly bear"

Moths

Cinnabar ▶
Sometimes flies by day, but weakly. Striped larvae feed in groups on ragwort. Common on waste ground and railway banks.
W.S. 40-45 mm.

Ragwort

Larva inside tree trunk

◀ Goat
Widespread, but well camouflaged and rarely seen. Larva eats wood of ash and willow. Spends three or four years in a tree trunk and pupates in a silk-bonded cocoon made of wood shavings. Larva smells like goats.
W.S. 70-85 mm.

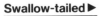

Swallow-tailed ▶
Looks like a butterfly. Weak, fluttering flight. Stick-like larva feeds on leaves of ivy, hawthorn, sloe, etc.
W.S. 56 mm.

Moths

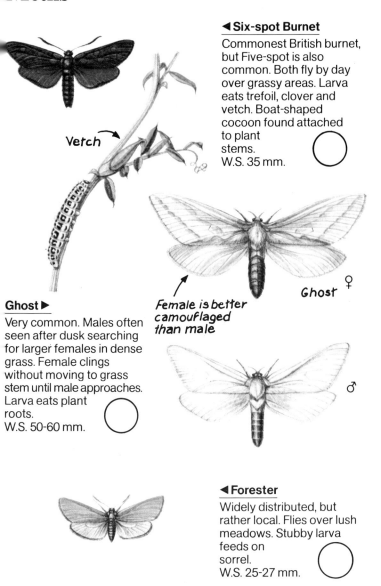

◀ Six-spot Burnet
Commonest British burnet, but Five-spot is also common. Both fly by day over grassy areas. Larva eats trefoil, clover and vetch. Boat-shaped cocoon found attached to plant stems.
W.S. 35 mm.

Vetch

Female is better camouflaged than male

Ghost ♀

Ghost ▶
Very common. Males often seen after dusk searching for larger females in dense grass. Female clings without moving to grass stem until male approaches. Larva eats plant roots.
W.S. 50-60 mm.

♂

◀ Forester
Widely distributed, but rather local. Flies over lush meadows. Stubby larva feeds on sorrel.
W.S. 25-27 mm.

279

Beetles

Most beetles have a pair of hard wing cases called elytra. There are several thousand species of beetles in Europe and their size varies enormously.

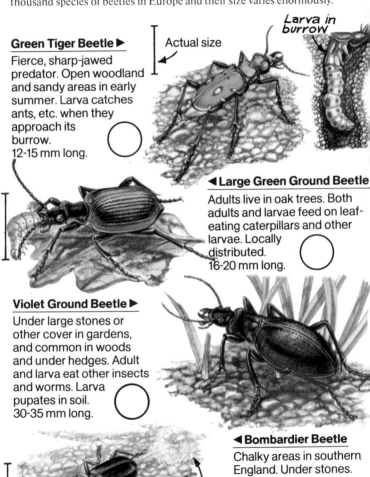

Green Tiger Beetle ▶

Fierce, sharp-jawed predator. Open woodland and sandy areas in early summer. Larva catches ants, etc. when they approach its burrow.
12-15 mm long.

Actual size

Larva in burrow

◀ Large Green Ground Beetle

Adults live in oak trees. Both adults and larvae feed on leaf-eating caterpillars and other larvae. Locally distributed.
16-20 mm long.

Violet Ground Beetle ▶

Under large stones or other cover in gardens, and common in woods and under hedges. Adult and larva eat other insects and worms. Larva pupates in soil.
30-35 mm long.

◀ Bombardier Beetle

Chalky areas in southern England. Under stones. Shoots irritating gas from end of its abdomen with a popping sound when threatened.
7-10 mm long.

Gas shooting from abdomen

Beetles

Devil's Coach Horse
or Cocktail Beetle ▶

Common in gardens. When challenged, raises tail and spreads jaws. Can ooze poisonous liquid from end of abdomen. Eats insect larvae, snails, slugs, etc. 25-30 mm long.

Larva

◀ Rove Beetle

Feeds mainly on dead animals and birds. Most common in southern England. Related to Devil's Coach Horse. 20 mm long.

Red and Black Burying Beetle ▶

Feeds on dead animals, kneading and biting the flesh and then burying the body. Female lays eggs in burrow beside the body. Larvae feed on it and pupate in a chamber in soil. 15-20 mm long.

Mouse

◀ Ant Beetle

Small, fast-moving beetle found on elms and conifers. Larvae live under loose bark. Adults and larvae eat larvae of bark beetles. 7-10 mm long.

Beetles

Great Diving Beetle ▶

Lakes and large ponds. Eats tadpoles, small fishes and other insects. Collects air from surface and stores it between wing covers and end of abdomen. 30-35 mm long.

Male's wing cases are smoother than female's

Larva

♀

◀ Great Silver Water Beetle

Largest British water beetle. Eats mainly water plants, but larva is a predator and eats water snails. Can fly to other waters if its home dries up. 37-48 mm long.

Carries bubble of air under body ↗

Whirligig Beetle ▶

Seen in groups on surface of ponds, lakes and slow rivers in bright sunshine. Darts in all directions. Carnivorous, eating mosquito larvae, etc. 6-8 mm long.

◀ Water Beetle

Lives among vegetation of lakes and rivers where it lays its eggs. Colour may be darker, sometimes all black. Widespread. 7-8 mm long.

Beetles

Glow-worm ▶

Grassy banks, hillsides, open woods. Most common in S. England. Wingless female attracts male with her glowing tail.
Male 15 mm long.
Female 20 mm long.

♀

Larva

♂

◀ Lesser Glow-worm

Near streams and on damp grassy banks. Like Glow-worm, male and larva have small lights on tip of abdomen. C. and S. Europe, but not found in Britain.
8-10 mm long.

♂

♀

Scarlet-tipped Flower Beetle ▶

Most common in southern England. In buttercups and other flower heads. Blows up scarlet bladders on its underside when handled.
7-10 mm long.

Buttercup

Larva is called "wireworm"

◀ Click Beetle or Skipjack

Local in dense vegetation or in flowers. Larvae live in soil, eating plant roots; other species of click beetle do much damage to crops.
14-18 mm long.

Larva

Beetles

Two-spot Ladybird ▶
Very common. Colour pattern often varies and some individuals are shiny black with red spots. 4-5 mm long.

Ladybird eating aphid

Rose

◀ Seven-spot Ladybird
Very common. Hibernates in large numbers in sheds, houses or tree bark. Emerges on sunny spring days to find aphids and lay its eggs. 6-7 mm long.

Eyed Ladybird ▶
Largest ladybird in Britain. Found near or on fir trees. Both adults and larvae hunt for aphids and scale-insects. 8-9 mm long.

Fir

Pattern varies

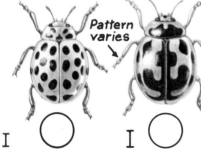

◀ 22-spot Ladybird (left)
◀ 14-spot Ladybird (right)
22-spot is found in many areas and habitats. 2-3 mm long. 14-spot is rare in the north. Trees and bushes. 3-4 mm long.

Beetles

Death Watch Beetle ▶
Larva eats timber in barns. The sound the adult makes when it taps its head against its tunnel walls was once believed to predict a death.
7-10 mm long.

◀ Cardinal Beetle
One of three species of cardinal beetles found in Britain. On flowers and under bark. Whitish larvae feed on bark and wood.
15-17 mm long.

Oil Beetle ▶
Flightless. Larva waits in a flower for a special kind of solitary bee to carry it to its nest where the larva feeds and grows. Local.
15-30 mm long.

◀ Blister Beetle
Rare. Name comes from a fluid in the insect's blood which causes blisters on human skin. Larvae live in mining bees' nests as parasites.
12-20 mm long.

Beetles

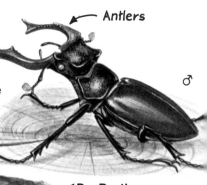

Antlers

Stag Beetle ▶

Largest British beetle.
Only male has antlers. Larvae
feed on tree stumps for
three years or more. Most
common in the south,
particularly Kent
and Surrey.
25-75 mm long.

♂

◀ Dor Beetle

Common. Seen flying
at night to dung heaps
where it lays its eggs.
Makes a loud droning
sound when it
flies.
16-24 mm long.

Horned Dung Beetle
or Minotaur Beetle ▶

In sandy places where
rabbits live. Eats their dung
and fills tunnels with it
for larvae
to eat. Local.
12-18 mm long.

◀ Cockchafer or May Bug

Common. Flies round
tree tops in early summer
and sometimes down
chimneys and at lighted
windows. Larvae may be
dug up in
gardens.
25-30 mm long.

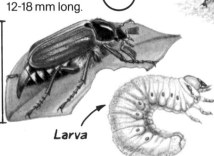

Larva

Beetles

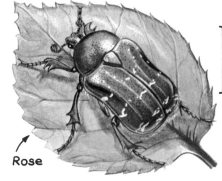

Rose Chafer ▶

Sometimes found in rose blooms and other flowers. Larvae feed on old timber and roots. Found all over Britain, but localized.
14-20 mm long.

Rose

◀ Bee Beetle

Mainly in Scotland and Wales. Found in flowers. Mimics colouring of bees. Larvae eat rotting wood, especially birch.
10-13 mm long.

Hairy like a bee

Pignut

Long "horns"

Musk Beetle ▶

Longhorn beetles have long antennae, perhaps so they can recognize each other when they emerge from their pupae in wood tunnels.
20-32 mm long.

Willow

◀ Wasp Beetle

Harmless, but looks and behaves like a wasp. Flies in bright sunshine visiting flowers. Common throughout Britain.
15 mm long.

287

Beetles

Colorado Beetle ▶

Damages potato crops. Introduced by accident from America; some still appear from Europe. Tell the police if you spot one. 10-12 mm long.

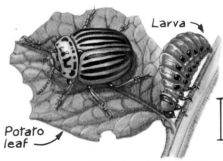

Larva ➤

Potato leaf ➤

Green Tortoise Beetle ▶

Legs and antennae often hidden so it looks like a tortoise. Well camouflaged on thistles where it feeds, and where larvae pupate. 6-8 mm long.

◀ Bloody-nosed Beetle

Like Oil and Blister Beetles, it reacts when threatened. It spurts bright red fluid from its mouth. This is called "reflex-bleeding". Low dense foliage. 10-20 mm long.

Mint ➤

Fork in larva's tail holds shed skins and droppings

◀ Nut Weevil

Female uses her long rostrum (or snout) to pierce a young hazel-nut where she lays her single egg. Larva grows inside the nut, eating the kernel. 10 mm long.

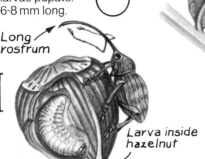

Long rostrum

Larva inside hazelnut

Bugs

Bugs might be confused with beetles, but their mouthparts are different. Bugs have a tube called a rostrum for piercing and sucking; beetles' mouthparts are adapted for biting, cutting and chewing.

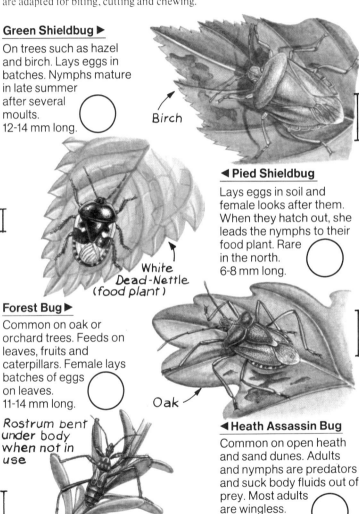

Green Shieldbug ▶

On trees such as hazel and birch. Lays eggs in batches. Nymphs mature in late summer after several moults.
12-14 mm long.

Birch

◀ Pied Shieldbug

Lays eggs in soil and female looks after them. When they hatch out, she leads the nymphs to their food plant. Rare in the north.
6-8 mm long.

White Dead-Nettle (food plant)

Forest Bug ▶

Common on oak or orchard trees. Feeds on leaves, fruits and caterpillars. Female lays batches of eggs on leaves.
11-14 mm long.

Oak

Rostrum bent under body when not in use

◀ Heath Assassin Bug

Common on open heath and sand dunes. Adults and nymphs are predators and suck body fluids out of prey. Most adults are wingless.
9-12 mm long.

Bugs

Water Cricket ▶

Common on still and slow-moving water. Runs on water surface eating insects and spiders. Lays eggs out of water on moss.
6-7 mm long.

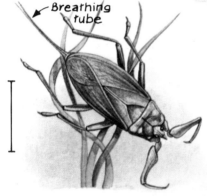

Breathing tube

Water Stick Insect ▶

Not related to true stick insects, but like them it is hard to see among plants. Most common in south Wales and southern England.
30-35 mm long.

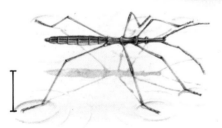

◀ Water Scorpion

Ponds and shallow lakes. Seizes small fishes, tadpoles, insect larvae with forelegs. Lays eggs in algae or on water plants.
18-22 mm long.

◀ Water Measurer

Edges of ponds and slow rivers and streams. Stabs at mosquito and larvae and water fleas with its rostrum. Also eats dead insects.
9-12 mm long.

Bugs

Water Boatman
or Backswimmer ▶

Pools, canals, ditches and water tanks. Jerks along with its hind legs, usually on its back. Eats tadpoles, small fishes, etc. Can fly away if its home dries up.
15 mm long.

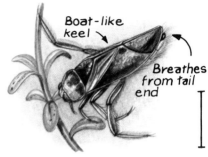

Boat-like keel ➘

Breathes from tail end

◀ Lesser Water Boatman

Flatter and rounder than Water Boatman and has shorter legs. Sucks up small bits of animal and plant material at bottom of ponds.
Common.
12-14 mm long.

Pond Skater ▶

Front legs adapted to catch dead or dying insects that fall on water surface. Some can fly; others have no wings. Common in ponds.
8-10 mm long.

◀ Saucer Bug

Lives in vegetation at bottom of muddy pools and canals. Like the Water Boatman it can stab you with its rostrum. Hibernates in winter as do most water bugs.
12-16 mm long.

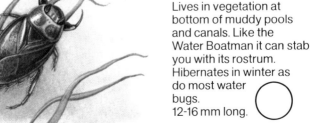

Bugs

New Forest Cicada ▶

Male makes high-pitched buzzing sound that is very difficult to hear. Nymphs live underground for several years eating plant roots. The only British cicada. 25 mm long.

Adult sucks sap from trees

Birch

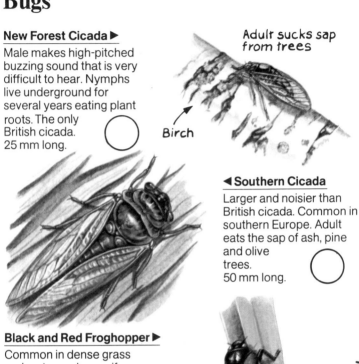

◀ Southern Cicada

Larger and noisier than British cicada. Common in southern Europe. Adult eats the sap of ash, pine and olive trees. 50 mm long.

Black and Red Froghopper ▶

Common in dense grass and on trees. Jumps if disturbed. Larvae secrete froth which covers them when they feed underground. 9-10 mm long.

Bracken

◀ Horned Treehopper

Tree branches and low vegetation, such as bracken, in woods. Adult and larva feed on oak leaves and other plants. 9-10 mm long.

Bugs

Eared Leafhopper ▶

On lichen-covered oak or other trees where it is well hidden. Adults appear about June. Moves slowly. Local in southern England. 13-17 mm long.

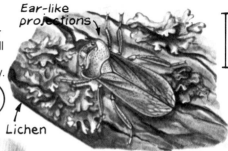

Ear-like projections

Lichen

◀ Green Leafhopper

Common throughout Britain. Feeds on grasses and rushes often in damp meadows and marshy places. 6-9 mm long.

Rose Aphid or Greenfly ▶

Green or pinkish. Feeds on roses in spring, then moves to other plants. Excretes honeydew which ants feed on. Pest on roses. 2-3 mm long.

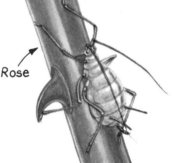

Rose

◀ Bean Aphid or Blackfly

Common on broad bean, but also on thistle and other plants. Lays eggs on spindle trees. Adults from these produce fully-formed young which eat beans. 2-3 mm long.

293

Dragonflies and Damselflies

Hawker dragonflies fly fast and hover and turn in the air. Darters fly in short, sharp bursts. Dragonflies, damselflies and their nymphs are carnivorous. They have very large compound eyes for spotting prey.

Emperor Dragonfly ▶

Largest British hawker. Large ponds, lakes and canals in summer. Adult catches flies, etc. in flight.
W.S. 105 mm.
80 mm long.

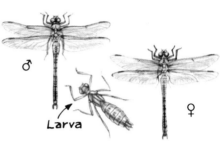

♂

Larva

♀

◀ Golden-ringed Dragonfly

Near streams and rivers, but like many dragonflies it is sometimes seen far from water. Female lays eggs in mud.
W.S. 100 mm.
75-85 mm long.

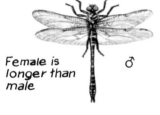

Female is longer than male

♂

Broad-bodied Libellula ▶

Ponds and lakes, particularly in southern England. Darters have shorter wings and stubbier bodies than hawkers. They fly in short sharp bursts.
W.S. 75 mm.
45 mm long.

♂

♀

◀ Downy Emerald

This darter flies fast over sluggish streams, rivers, ponds and lakes in summer. Quite common in S. England.
W.S. 68 mm.
48 mm long.

♂

Dragonflies

Ruddy Sympetrum ▶

Weedy ponds or ditches
in marshy areas. Nymphs
mature more quickly than
the larger dragonflies
which may take
2-3 years.
W.S. 55 mm.
35 mm long.

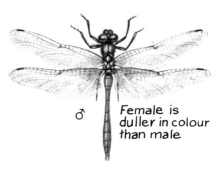

♂

*Female is
duller in colour
than male*

♀

◀ Demoiselle Agrion

Fast-flowing clear streams
with sandy or stony
bottoms. Damselflies
usually rest with wings
together, not spread out
like dragonflies.
W.S. 58-63 mm.
45 mm long.

Banded Agrion ▶

More common than the
Demoiselle but rare in
northern England and not
recorded from Scotland.
Usually by streams and
rivers with
muddy bottoms.
W.S. 60-65 mm.
45 mm long.

♂

♂

♀

◀ Common Ischnura or
Blue-tailed Damselfly

On plants by ditches,
canals, lakes, ponds and
slow-moving rivers and
streams. Common in most
of Britain.
W.S. 35 mm.
30 mm long.

♂

Bees and Wasps

Bees, wasps and ants belong to the same order. Some species are "social insects" and colonies of these include queens, drones and workers. Other insects in this order are solitary and have no caste system.

Red-tailed Bumblebee ▶

Common in gardens. Queen makes a nest in a hole in the ground. Eggs develop into colonies of queens, workers and drones. Queen is 22 mm long.

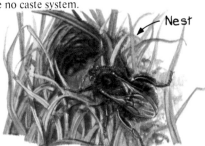

Nest

◀ Leaf-cutter Bee

Cuts semi-circular pieces from rose leaves to make cylinders where the female lays a single egg provided with nectar and pollen. Solitary species. Male 10 mm long. Female 11 mm.

Leaves cut by bee

Potter Wasp ▶

Makes pots of clay for its larvae. Each larva has a separate pot, stocked with small caterpillars (paralyzed with a sting) for food. Sandy heaths. Male 12 mm long. Female 14 mm.

Pot

◀ Sand Wasp

Makes a nest burrow in sand where it lays a single egg on top of a paralyzed caterpillar. Larva eats the caterpillar. 28-30 mm long.

Wasps

Ruby-tailed Wasp ▶

Called a "cuckoo-wasp" because female lays egg in nest of a solitary bee or wasp. When larva hatches it eats host's food and its egg or larva. 12 mm long.

◀ Velvet Ant

Actually a wasp, but female is wingless. She lays her egg in a bee larva which is eaten by her own larva when it hatches. Can sting painfully. 15 mm long.

♀

Ichneumon Fly ▶

A wasp, not a fly. Female pierces pine trees with her ovipositor (egg layer) and lays an egg on a Horntail larva or in its burrow inside the tree. 22-30 mm long.

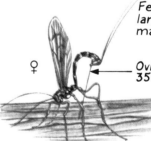

♀

Female is larger than male

Ovipositor is 35 mm long

♂

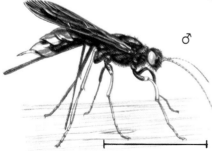

◀ Giant Wood Wasp or Horntail

Female lays eggs in sickly or felled conifers. Larvae feed on wood for up to three years. 25-32 mm long.

Wasps

Blue Horntail ▶

Male like male Horntail except his head, thorax and the first two segments of his abdomen are deep metallic blue. Female is all blue and has only a short ovipositor. 20-25 mm long.

Dog rose

Brown and yellow markings

◀ Hornet

Not as likely to sting as the Common Wasp. Nests in hollow trees, banks or roofs. Preys on soft-bodied insects with which it feeds its larvae. Also feeds from flowers in woods. 22-30 mm long.

German Wasp ▶

With the Common Wasp, Britain's commonest species. Most troublesome in late summer when the larvae are mature. 15-20 mm long.

Marmalade

Wasp's nest in tree

◀ Tree Wasp

Likes to nest in woods, often hanging its oval nest from a tree branch. More locally distributed than Common or German Wasps. 15-20 mm long.

Ants

Carpenter Ant ▶

Hollows out pine tree trunks where it nests, often making the tree fall down.
Not in Britain.
8-18 mm long.

Nest tunnel

Actual size of worker ant

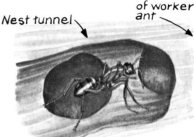

I

Nest

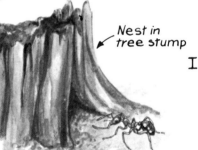

◀ Wood Ant

Makes large conical nest from twigs and leaves in pine woods. Useful to foresters as it eats leaf-eating larvae. Cannot sting, but sprays formic acid at intruders.
5-11 mm long.

Red Ant ▶

Nests under stones or in rotting wood. Rears aphids in its nest and feeds on their honeydew.
3-6 mm long.

Nest in tree stump

I

I

◀ Black Ant

Common in gardens. Like all ants, only queens and males have wings. Males die after mating and queens start a new colony.
3-9 mm long.

Ant, Sawfly, Gall-wasps

Yellow Meadow Ant ▶

Makes small mounds in meadows. Sometimes "farms" other small insects, such as aphids, for a sugary liquid that they excrete.
2-9 mm long.

I

Actual size of worker ant

Sawfly larva has nine pairs of legs. Moth larvae have eight pairs

◀ Birch Sawfly

Name "sawfly" comes from female's saw-like ovipositor. Larva feeds on birch leaves in late summer. It makes a large oval cocoon and the adult emerges the next spring.
20-23 mm long.

Oak Marble Gall-wasp ▶

Female lays egg in leaf bud. Larva's feeding causes the tree to "blister" round it. Only one larva lives in each "marble".
4 mm long.

Marble gall

I

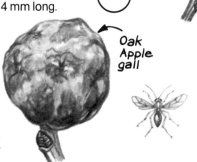

Oak Apple gall

I

◀ Oak Apple Gall-wasp

These galls can be 40 mm across and are at first red and green and then later darken. Each gall contains many larvae. Insect is 3 mm long.

300

True Flies

True flies have only one pair of wings. The second pair are replaced by two halteres which are like tiny drumsticks. Flies probably use them for balance. The insects that appear on pages 304-306 are not true flies, but belong to different orders.

Grey Flesh Fly ▶

Common. Lays eggs in carrion. White, legless larvae (maggots) feed on flesh before turning into oval brown pupae.
6-17 mm long.

Rat

◀ Greenbottle Fly

Most species lay eggs in carrion. Adults seen on flowers. One species lays eggs in skin or fleece of sheep and its larvae eat the sheep's flesh.
7-11 mm long.

Mouse

Drone Fly ▶

Makes a loud, bee-like droning in flight. Visits flowers for nectar and pollen. Larva rests on the pond bottom and breathes through a long tube.
15 mm long.

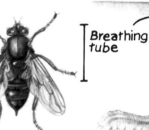

Breathing tube

Antirrhinum

◀ Hover Fly

Hovers as though motionless. Common in summer. Female lays eggs among aphids and the legless larvae eat them.
10-14 mm long.

True Flies

Dung Fly ▶

Visits fresh cowpats where female lays eggs. Rise in a buzzing mass if disturbed but soon settle again. Larvae eat dung but adults are predators on other flies. 10-12 mm long.

Cow pat

◀ Robber Fly

Preys on other insects by capturing them and sucking out their body fluids. Larvae feed on animal dung as well as vegetable matter. 18-26 mm long.

Robber-fly killing damsel fly

Bee Fly ▶

Probes flowers in gardens for nectar in spring. Lays eggs near nests of mining bees and its larvae eat the bee's larvae. Most common in S. England. 10-11 mm long.

Sweet woodruff

◀ Horse Fly

Female sucks blood but her loud hum warns you before you get bitten. Smaller species are more silent and stab before being noticed. Found in old forests in S. England. 20-25 mm long.

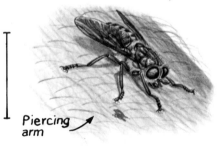

Piercing arm

True Flies

Fever Fly ▶
Does not bite or cause fever. Most noticeable in spring and summer. Males perform courtship dance in the air above females. 8 mm long.

Water violet

Larva

◀ Giant Cranefly or Daddy-long-legs
Often near water. Other species found in gardens where larvae (called "leatherjackets") eat root crops and grass roots. 30-40 mm long.

Black and Yellow Cranefly ▶
Low vegetation. Craneflies mate end to end and can be seen joined like this in summer. Female lays eggs in soil with her pointed ovipositor. 18-20 mm long.

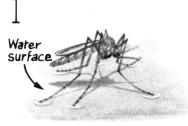
Water surface

◀ Common Gnat or Mosquito
Sucks birds' blood, but not people's. Lays eggs in raft-like clusters which float on water. Larvae hang down below surface. 6-7 mm long.

303

Ant-lion, Lacewings

Ant–lion ▶
Name refers to larva which traps ants and other insects in a sandy hollow. Grabs them in its sickle-like jaws and sucks them dry.
Not in Britain.
Adult 35 mm long.

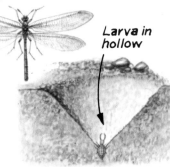

Larva in hollow

Body length

◀ Giant Lacewing
Mainly nocturnal. Larvae eat small midge larvae they find in wet moss at water's edge. Pupate in silken yellowish cocoons.
15 mm long.

Green Lacewing ▶
Gardens and hedges and sometimes attracted to house lights. Weak fluttering flight. Larvae feed on aphids.
15 mm long.

Larva catching aphid

◀ Brown Lacewing
Smaller than Green Lacewing with dark brownish transparent wings. Near water in lush vegetation and on trees.
Throughout Britain.
10 mm long.

Scorpion Fly, Alder Fly, Snake Fly

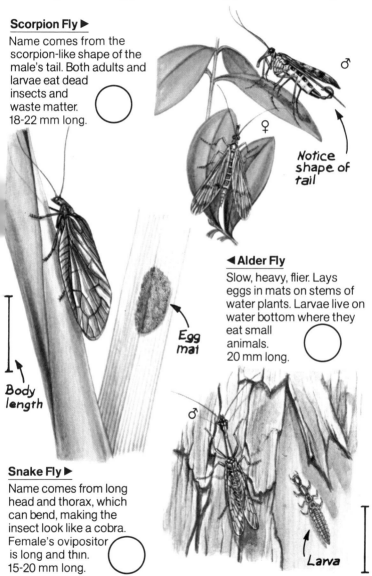

Scorpion Fly ▶
Name comes from the scorpion-like shape of the male's tail. Both adults and larvae eat dead insects and waste matter. 18-22 mm long.

♂

♀

Notice shape of tail

Body length

◀ Alder Fly
Slow, heavy, flier. Lays eggs in mats on stems of water plants. Larvae live on water bottom where they eat small animals. 20 mm long.

Egg mat

♂

Larva

Snake Fly ▶
Name comes from long head and thorax, which can bend, making the insect look like a cobra. Female's ovipositor is long and thin. 15-20 mm long.

Caddis Fly, Stonefly, Mayfly

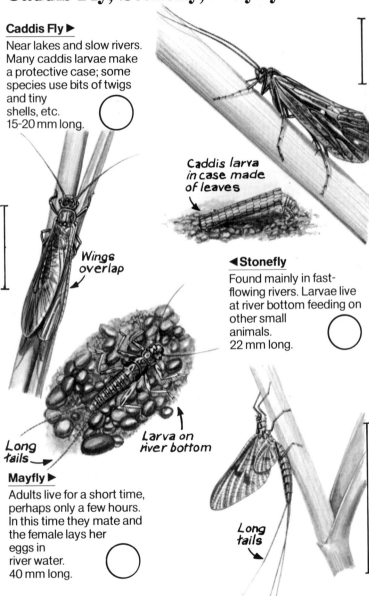

Caddis Fly ▶

Near lakes and slow rivers. Many caddis larvae make a protective case; some species use bits of twigs and tiny shells, etc. 15-20 mm long.

Caddis larva in case made of leaves

Wings overlap

◀ Stonefly

Found mainly in fast-flowing rivers. Larvae live at river bottom feeding on other small animals. 22 mm long.

Long tails

Larva on river bottom

Mayfly ▶

Adults live for a short time, perhaps only a few hours. In this time they mate and the female lays her eggs in river water. 40 mm long.

Long tails

Crickets

Crickets and bush crickets have very long antennae; grasshoppers' antennae are short. The third pair of legs on these insects is adapted for leaping. Males "sing" to attract females by rubbing their wing-cases together. The praying mantis, stick insect and cockroach belong to different orders.

Field Cricket ▶
Very rare. Grassy banks and meadows in sandy or chalky areas. Male sings from his burrow to attract a female.
Flightless.
20 mm long.

◀ House Cricket
In heated buildings and greenhouses. Also occurs in garden rubbish heaps and bigger tips.
Rarely flies.
Shrill song.
16 mm long.

Wood Cricket ▶
In leaf litter in woodland rides, ditches and banks in southern England. Male has quiet churring song. Flightless.
8-9 mm long.

◀ Mole Cricket
Burrows like a mole with its large spade-like fore-feet. Damp meadows. Male makes continuous whirring call.
Rare.
38-42 mm long.

Bush Crickets, Grasshopper

Great Green Bush Cricket ▶

Harsh, shrill, penetrating
song. Moves slowly and
never flies far. Eats small
insects which it
finds in dense
vegetation.
45-47 mm long.

◀ Wart-biter

May bite when handled.
Swedish people once
used it to bite their warts.
Coarse grassland on
downs. Preys on
small insects.
34-35 mm long.

Speckled Bush Cricket ▶

Flightless adults seen in
late summer or early
autumn. Found in old
gardens where shrubs
grow. Males' song
is hard to hear.
11-13 mm long.

*Long
hind
legs*

*Wings look silvery
in flight*

◀ Large Marsh Grasshopper

Local in bog and fenland
in S. England, Norfolk
Broads and Ireland. Flies a
long way when disturbed.
Male makes slow
ticking song.
27-32 mm long.

Cockroaches, Mantis

Common Cockroach ▶

In houses and other warm buildings, where it eats waste. Female lays eggs in purse-like containers. Does not fly.
25 mm long.

Old bread

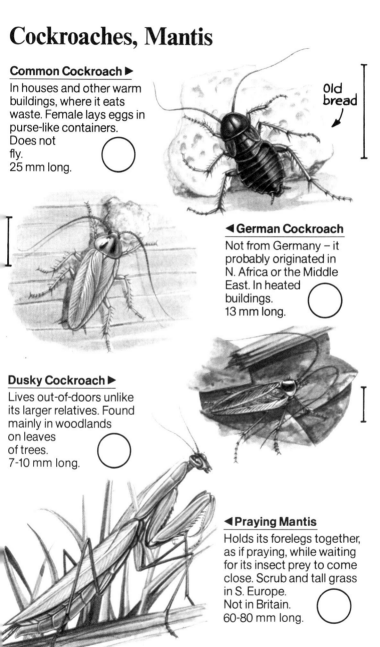

◀ German Cockroach

Not from Germany – it probably originated in N. Africa or the Middle East. In heated buildings.
13 mm long.

Dusky Cockroach ▶

Lives out-of-doors unlike its larger relatives. Found mainly in woodlands on leaves of trees.
7-10 mm long.

◀ Praying Mantis

Holds its forelegs together, as if praying, while waiting for its insect prey to come close. Scrub and tall grass in S. Europe.
Not in Britain.
60-80 mm long.

Stick Insect, Earwigs

Stick Insect ▶

Lives in bushes in S. Europe. Eats vegetation. Not in Britain. Another species, the Laboratory Stick Insect, is often kept as a pet. Up to 90 mm long.

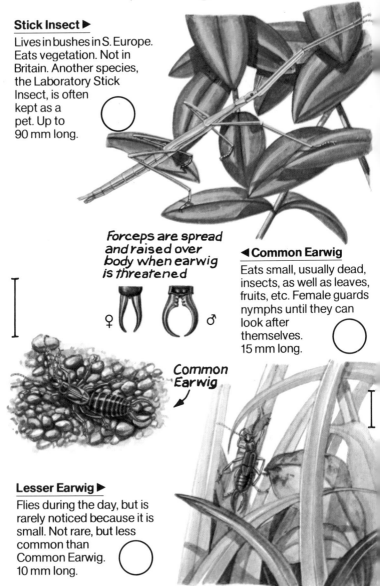

Forceps are spread and raised over body when earwig is threatened

♀   ♂

◀ Common Earwig

Eats small, usually dead, insects, as well as leaves, fruits, etc. Female guards nymphs until they can look after themselves. 15 mm long.

Common Earwig

Lesser Earwig ▶

Flies during the day, but is rarely noticed because it is small. Not rare, but less common than Common Earwig. 10 mm long.

Chapter 7
MAMMALS

Introduction to Chapter 7

Chapter Seven will help you to identify more than 50 species of mammals and the tracks they leave. Next to each picture of an animal there is a description of some of its main characteristics, its habitat and size. Most of the measurements given are average sizes. The hoofed mammals have been measured from the top of the shoulder to the bottom of the hoof – this is their shoulder height (SH). The rest of the mammals are measured from the nose to the rump – this is called the head and body length (H&B).

An outline of the track made by each animal is next to its picture. The dark brown areas represent the pads and claws and any bright yellow represents webbing between the toes. Animal tracks are usually measured lengthwise.

Length of track

Head and body length

European Mink

Pony

Shoulder height

Looking for mammals and tracks

The best times to go out are in the early morning and evening when the animals are active. Choose a quiet spot away from human activity. If you find burrows and holes go back to them in the early evening when the animals come out to feed.

Test which way the wind is blowing and walk into the wind so that the animal does not catch your scent. Keep to trees and bushes and move quietly and slowly; do not make any sudden movements. Do not walk along a ridge, because the animals will see your outline against the sky.

The tracks shown in this book are perfect ones, but the tracks you will find may be only partly complete, or distorted by thawing

Badger tracks in snow

snow or uneven ground. You will have to interpret the patterns and train yourself to look for other clues. The size of the track may confuse you if it has been made by a young animal. Tracks made by fore and hind feet may look different and a track made in mud will look very different to one made in snow or sand.

Mammal homes below ground

Inside an underground burrow a mammal can keep warm and rear its young in safety. Signs outside the entrance, such as droppings or tracks, may tell you who lives inside; you should be able to guess the size of the owner from the size of the opening.

Each mammal has its own way of removing waste earth from the burrow. The Fox throws earth out of the entrance, leaving it in a fan-shaped pile; the Wood Mouse leaves a conical pile; the Mole pushes waste soil up onto the surface and the Water Vole presses it against the side of the burrow.

▲ **Molehills.** Made of waste earth from mole tunnels. The sleeping nest will be under the largest hill, called the fortress; this pile of earth may be over 30 cm high. The breeding nest will have no hill over it.

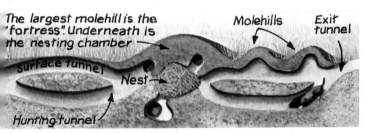

The largest molehill is the 'fortress'. Underneath is the nesting chamber

surface tunnel

Nest

Hunting tunnel

Molehills

Exit tunnel

▲ **Fox's den.** Look for the heap of earth outside. There may be tracks or droppings on the earth and a strong smell inside the hole. Foxes often use badger sets or dig out old rabbit burrows. A single Fox, or a family of Foxes may live in each den. They may move dens.

Badger's set ▲ There may be remains of bedding outside the main entrance; other openings will be nearby. There is no smell inside the set and droppings are left in shallow holes outside. A group of Badgers will live in one set.

Mammal homes above ground

Most hoofed animals do not have permanent homes. They sleep on the ground in sheltered places. The sleeping places of deer are called lairs; the vegetation here will be flattened and there may be droppings nearby. The Roe Deer scrapes away plants and twigs with its hooves before lying down. Other mammals, such as dormice, build nests in vegetation. The nests are well hidden and keep the animal warm and dry when it is sleeping. Different nests may be built in winter and summer; a nest which is used for breeding will be lined with soft material.

Old nests are easier to see in winter when the vegetation has died back. During breeding time, the activity of the parents popping in and out of the nest to feed young may lead you to the nest site. Do not remove any empty nests you find; they may be used.

The drey is 20-50 cm wide

The nest is 8-10 cm wide

Grey Squirrel's drey ▲ Made of twigs, lined with moss, grass, feathers and fur. Looks like a large, round bird's nest in the fork of a tree; a simple summer drey may be built on side branches. ◯

▲ Harvest Mouse's summer nest
Made of grass leaves woven around long grass or reed stems, high off the ground; sometimes in bushes.
In winter, nests are in small tunnels, or under rocks or roots. ◯

The nest is 8 cm wide

The form is 40 cm long

Dormouse's winter nest ▲ Made of plant material, mainly strips of bark. Found in thick undergrowth, often close to the ground, or in bushes especially hazel; sometimes in bird nesting boxes. ◯

▲ Hare's form. A shallow hollow scraped away in earth, grass or snow, usually protected at the side by a clump of grass or a stone. The Hare sits with its hindquarters in the deepest part of the form. ◯

Deer

Hoofed animals are called ungulates. Most European ungulates, like deer, walk on two toes and leave two-toed tracks; the horse, however, walks on one toe. Deer have branched antlers which they drop after the rut, while cattle, sheep and goats have unbranched horns which are never lost.

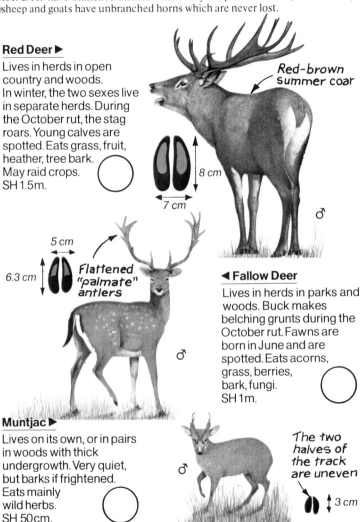

Red Deer ▶

Lives in herds in open country and woods. In winter, the two sexes live in separate herds. During the October rut, the stag roars. Young calves are spotted. Eats grass, fruit, heather, tree bark. May raid crops. SH 1.5m.

Red-brown summer coat

8 cm

7 cm

♂

5 cm

6.3 cm

Flattened "palmate" antlers

♂

◀ Fallow Deer

Lives in herds in parks and woods. Buck makes belching grunts during the October rut. Fawns are born in June and are spotted. Eats acorns, grass, berries, bark, fungi. SH 1m.

Muntjac ▶

Lives on its own, or in pairs in woods with thick undergrowth. Very quiet, but barks if frightened. Eats mainly wild herbs. SH 50cm.

♂

The two halves of the track are uneven

3 cm

315

Deer

Roe Deer ▶

Red-brown in summer,
grey-brown in winter. Lives
on its own, or in small
groups in conifer wood
plantations, near water.
The rut is in July/August.
Eats leaves,
herbs, berries.
SH 70cm.

Tine

*There are
three tines
on each
antler*

5 cm
4 cm

♂

*Flattened,
palmate
antlers*

◀ Elk/Moose

Largest European deer.
In N. and E. Europe. Not in
Britain. In woods or
marshes. Lives on its own
in summer; in winter, lives
in herds. Swims well.
Eats water plants,
grass, moss.
SH 1.8m.

Beard

16 cm

12 cm

5 cm
8 cm

*Rarely more
than four tines
on each antler*

♂

Sika Deer ▶

Originally from Asia, but
found in British woods.
Hinds live in small groups.
Stags live on their own; the
make short, screaming
grunts during the October
rut. Eats bark, grass,
may raid crops.
SH 80cm.

Deer, Sheep

Reindeer ▶

Coat colour varies; both
sexes have antlers. Lives in
herds in mountains and
tundra of N. Scandinavia;
a herd has been introduced
into Scotland. Swims well.
Hooves make a clacking
sound when it is walking.
Eats "reindeer
moss" (a lichen).
SH 1.1m.

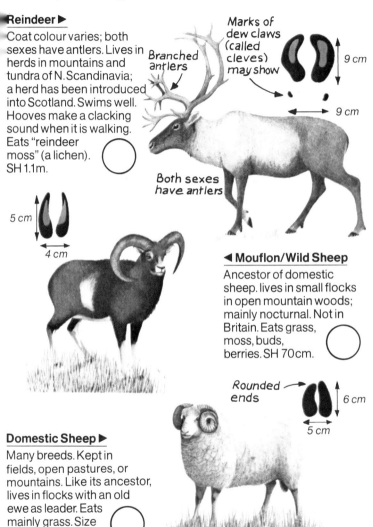

Branched antlers

Marks of dew claws (called cleves) may show

9 cm

9 cm

Both sexes have antlers

5 cm

4 cm

◀ Mouflon/Wild Sheep

Ancestor of domestic
sheep. lives in small flocks
in open mountain woods;
mainly nocturnal. Not in
Britain. Eats grass,
moss, buds,
berries. SH 70 cm.

Rounded ends

6 cm

5 cm

Domestic Sheep ▶

Many breeds. Kept in
fields, open pastures, or
mountains. Like its ancestor,
lives in flocks with an old
ewe as leader. Eats
mainly grass. Size
varies with breed.

Goats, Chamois

Domestic Goat ▶

Many breeds. Wild on mountains, or domestic on farms. Male is called a billy and usually has a beard. Size varies.

Size varies with the breed

♂

Similar to sheep tracks (more rounded than deer tracks)

9 cm

5 cm

Horns up to 1m long

Coat is shaggy in winter

◀ Ibex/Wild Goat

Lives in flocks on high mountains in Europe. Not in Britain. Billy has a beard. Very agile. Eats grass, lichen, moss, leaves. SH 75 cm.

♂

Both sexes have horns

Chamois ▶

Both sexes have horns. Lives in flocks on wooded mountains. Not in Britain. Males live on their own. Very agile. Eats grass, berries, buds. SH 75cm.

6 cm

3.5 cm

Otter, Martens

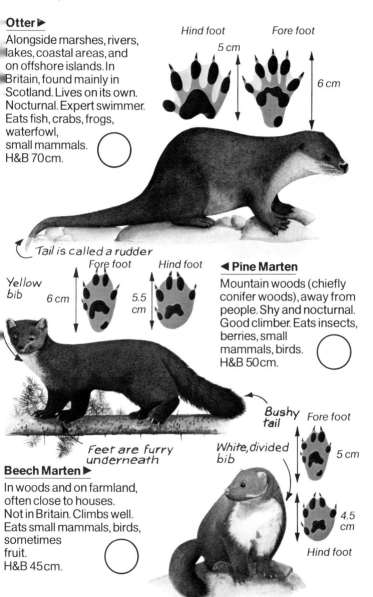

Otter ▶

Alongside marshes, rivers, lakes, coastal areas, and on offshore islands. In Britain, found mainly in Scotland. Lives on its own. Nocturnal. Expert swimmer. Eats fish, crabs, frogs, waterfowl, small mammals. H&B 70 cm.

Hind foot 5 cm   *Fore foot* 6 cm

Tail is called a rudder

Yellow bib   *Fore foot* 6 cm   *Hind foot* 5.5 cm

◀ Pine Marten

Mountain woods (chiefly conifer woods), away from people. Shy and nocturnal. Good climber. Eats insects, berries, small mammals, birds. H&B 50 cm.

Bushy tail   Fore foot 5 cm

Feet are furry underneath

White, divided bib   4.5 cm   *Hind foot*

Beech Marten ▶

In woods and on farmland, often close to houses. Not in Britain. Climbs well. Eats small mammals, birds, sometimes fruit. H&B 45 cm.

Foxes, Badger

Red Fox ▶

Common on farmland and in woods, but also on mountains and in towns. Usually nocturnal. Catches small mammals, birds, poultry, young deer.
H&B 65cm.

Small pad

6 cm

5 cm

Fore foot   *Hind foot*

Winter coat

Tracks are 4.5 cm long and similar to those of the Red Fox

◀ Arctic Fox

On tundra and mountains in N. Scandinavia. Not in Britain. Smaller than Red Fox. Coat is dull brown in summer with no white tail tip; usually all white in winter, occasionally grey, Lives in small groups. Active by day and night. H&B 60cm.

Badger ▶

Mainly in woods, but also on mountains. Nocturnal. Lives in a large group in an underground set. Eats mainly worms; also small mammals, insect larvae, wasp nests, plants, roots.
H&B 80cm.

Kidney shaped pad

4 cm

5 cm
Fore foot

Hind foot

Stoat, Weasel, Mink, Polecat

Stoat ▶

Found in woods, farmland and on mountains. Northern stoats, called ermines, are white in winter; tip of tail is always black. Runs with an arched back. Eats rabbits, game birds, eggs. H&B 28 cm.

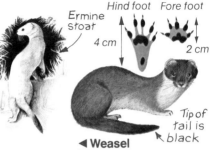

Ermine stoat

Hind foot   Fore foot
4 cm   2 cm

Tip of tail is black

◀ Weasel

Smaller than the stoat; found in similar areas, but prefers dry places. Not in Ireland. Nocturnal and inquisitive. Runs with an arched back. Eats small mammals, birds, eggs. H&B 20 cm.

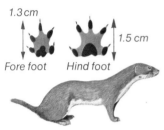

1.3 cm

1.5 cm

Fore foot   Hind foot

European Mink ▶

France and E. Europe. The American Mink has escaped from fur farms in Britain and Europe. Lives near water and swims well. Eats waterfowl, fish, frogs, small mammals, gamebirds, poultry. H&B 38 cm.

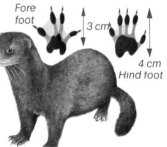

Fore foot

3 cm

4 cm
Hind foot

Upper lip is spotted with white

◀ Polecat

Wooded country, often near houses. Rare in Britain. Nocturnal. Tame ones are called ferrets and can be white; they often escape and live wild. Eats frogs, birds, rodents, rabbits. H&B 40 cm.

Dark face mask →

3 cm

5 cm
Hind foot

Fore foot

Beaver, Coypu, Muskrat

Most rodents are vegetarians and have many chewing teeth. The long, front teeth, called incisors, have sharp edges and are used for gnawing; they wear down easily, but grow continuously to make up for this.

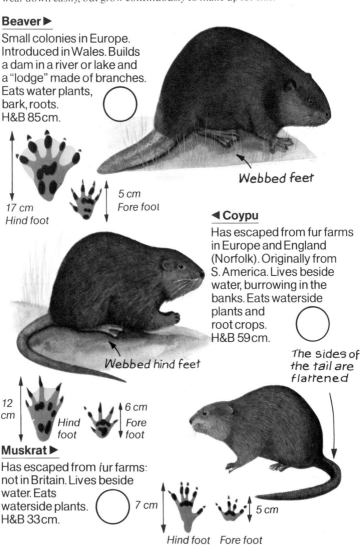

Beaver ▶

Small colonies in Europe. Introduced in Wales. Builds a dam in a river or lake and a "lodge" made of branches. Eats water plants, bark, roots. H&B 85 cm.

Webbed feet

17 cm
Hind foot

5 cm
Fore foot

◀ Coypu

Has escaped from fur farms in Europe and England (Norfolk). Originally from S. America. Lives beside water, burrowing in the banks. Eats waterside plants and root crops. H&B 59 cm.

The sides of the tail are flattened

Webbed hind feet

12 cm
Hind foot

6 cm
Fore foot

Muskrat ▶

Has escaped from fur farms: not in Britain. Lives beside water. Eats waterside plants. H&B 33 cm.

7 cm

Hind foot   Fore foot

5 cm

Squirrels, Dormouse

Red Squirrel ▶

Mostly in conifer woods.
Active by day, but shy. Eats
seeds of cones, berries,
buds, bark, birds'
eggs, nuts, fungi.
H&B 23 cm.

Ear tufts

Fore foot 3 cm *Hind foot 4 cm*

Hind foot 4 cm *Fore foot 3 cm*

◀ Grey Squirrel

Coat may have patches of
brown. Its habits are much
the same as the Red Squirrel,
but it is bolder and is
found in most woods,
parks and
gardens.
H&B 27 cm.

Fore foot 1.5 cm *Hind foot 2 cm*

Eyes are ringed with black

Edible Dormouse ▶

Introduced in Britain
(Hertfordshire). In deciduous
woods, parks and orchards.
May live near houses,
attracted by stored fruit.
Nocturnal. Hibernates in
winter. Eats nuts,
fruit, insects,
bark. H&B 12 cm.

Dormice, Hamster

Common Dormouse ▶

In Britain, lives in heavy undergrowth, copses and hedges. Honeysuckle bark is used to build its hibernation and breeding nests. Nocturnal and solitary; climbs well. Eats insects, berries, seeds, nuts. H&B 8cm.

Hind foot
1.5 cm

Fore foot
1 cm

◀ Garden Dormouse

Larger, with a more pointed face than the Common Dormouse, but its food and habits are the same. It may enter buildings. Not in Britain or Scandinavia. H&B 13cm.

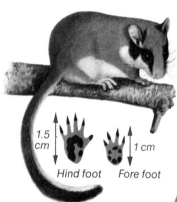

1.5 cm

1 cm

Hind foot   *Fore foot*

European Hamster ▶

Central Europe on open grassland. Not in Britain. Nocturnal. Lives on its own in a system of burrows. Hibernates. Carries food for storing in its cheek pouches. H&B 27 cm.

Hind foot   *Fore foot*

2.5 cm

2 cm

Marmot, Rats

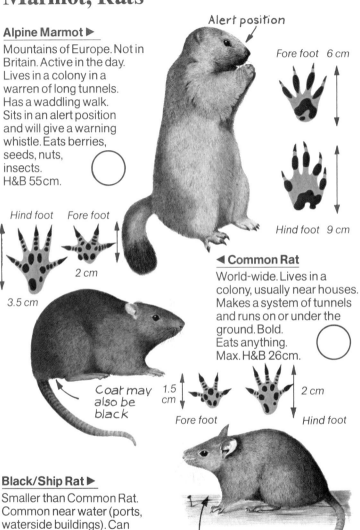

Alpine Marmot ▶

Mountains of Europe. Not in Britain. Active in the day. Lives in a colony in a warren of long tunnels. Has a waddling walk. Sits in an alert position and will give a warning whistle. Eats berries, seeds, nuts, insects.
H&B 55cm.

Alert position

Fore foot 6 cm

Hind foot 9 cm

Hind foot   Fore foot

3.5 cm   2 cm

◀ Common Rat

World-wide. Lives in a colony, usually near houses. Makes a system of tunnels and runs on or under the ground. Bold. Eats anything.
Max. H&B 26cm.

Coat may also be black

1.5 cm

Fore foot

2 cm

Hind foot

Black/Ship Rat ▶

Smaller than Common Rat. Common near water (ports, waterside buildings). Can climb well. Nocturnal and rather shy. Eats anything.
Max. H&B 20cm.

Coat may also be grey or grey-black

Voles, Lemming

Water Vole ▶

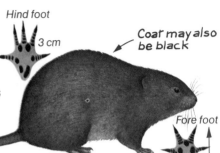

Hind foot
3 cm

Coat may also be black

Fore foot
2.5 cm

W. Europe. Not in Ireland. Active by day. Swims well and digs its burrows in the banks of ponds, canals, streams and marshes. Eats waterside plants, worms, snails, fish. H&B 19cm.

◀ Short-tailed/Field Vole

Not in Ireland. Widespread on open ground. Active by day. Rarely climbs, but makes tunnels through the undergrowth. Eats grass, roots, bark. H&B 11cm.

Short tail

Hind foot
1.2 cm

Fore foot
1 cm

Fore foot
1 cm

Hind foot
1.3 cm

Bank Vole ▶

Widespread in deciduous woods and hedgerows. Active by day. Climbs well and makes its burrows in banks. Eats buds, berries, insects, bark. H&B 10cm.

◀ Norway Lemming

Lives in colonies, usually on mountains. Not in Britain. Migrates in large groups every two or three years. Eats berries, grass, bark. H&B 14cm.

Very short tail

Hind foot
1.8 cm

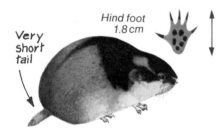

Mice

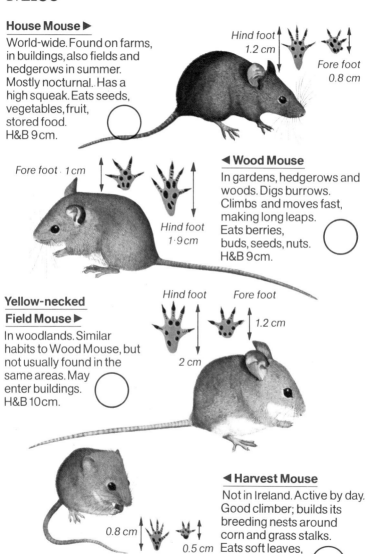

House Mouse ▶

World-wide. Found on farms, in buildings, also fields and hedgerows in summer. Mostly nocturnal. Has a high squeak. Eats seeds, vegetables, fruit, stored food. H&B 9 cm.

Hind foot 1.2 cm

Fore foot 0.8 cm

Fore foot · 1 cm

Hind foot 1·9 cm

◀ Wood Mouse

In gardens, hedgerows and woods. Digs burrows. Climbs and moves fast, making long leaps. Eats berries, buds, seeds, nuts. H&B 9 cm.

Yellow-necked Field Mouse ▶

In woodlands. Similar habits to Wood Mouse, but not usually found in the same areas. May enter buildings. H&B 10 cm.

Hind foot

Fore foot

1.2 cm

2 cm

0.8 cm

0.5 cm

Hind foot   Fore foot

◀ Harvest Mouse

Not in Ireland. Active by day. Good climber; builds its breeding nests around corn and grass stalks. Eats soft leaves, insects, seeds. H&B 6 cm.

327

Rabbit, Hares

Rabbit ▶

On farm and woodland, sand dunes and hillsides. Lives in colonies in a large burrow system. Active dusk and dawn. Thumps the ground with its hind feet when alarmed. Eats plants. H&B 40cm.

Fore foot   *Hind foot*

2.5 cm

12 cm

3 cm   13 cm

Fore foot   *Hind foot*

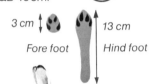

Winter coat

Summer coat

◀ Blue Hare

Mountainous country in Britain, Scandinavia and the Alps. Lives on its own. Active by day and night. Rests above ground and eats mountain plants. H&B 50cm.

Fore foot   *Hind foot*

3.5 cm

15 cm

Long ears

It has longer legs than a rabbit

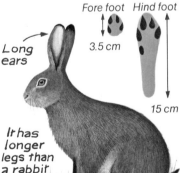

Brown Hare ▶

Lives on open farmland and woodland. Not in Norway, Sweden or most of Ireland. Usually solitary and silent. Rests above ground in a hollow ("form"). H&B 58cm.

Shrews

Common Shrew ▶

Rough pasture, woods, hedgerows, dunes and marshes. Not in Ireland. Climbs and swims. Has a high, shrill squeak. Very quarrelsome. Eats insects, worms. H&B 7 cm.

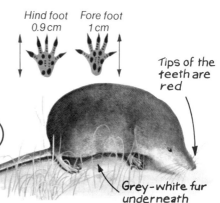

Hind foot 0.9 cm

Fore foot 1 cm

Tips of the teeth are red

Grey-white fur underneath

Hind foot 1.4 cm

Fore foot 1.2 cm

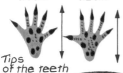

Tips of the teeth are red

◀ Water Shrew

Not in Ireland. Lives close to water; makes tunnels in the banks. A good swimmer; active day and night. Eats small fish, worms, insects. H&B 8 cm.

Tips of the teeth are red

Pygmy Shrew ▶

In dry undergrowth of hedges, young conifer woods, heather and rough pasture. Habits are similar to those of the Common Shrew. H&B 5 cm.

Hind foot 0.5 cm

Fore foot 0.4 cm

Mole, Hedgehog, Shrew

Mole ▶

Lives underground on farms and in woods. Not in Ireland. Does not burrow in sandy or marshy areas. Occasionally comes to the surface. Molehills are piles of waste earth from its tunnels. Sensitive to vibrations. Eats grubs, earthworms, insects. H&B 13cm.

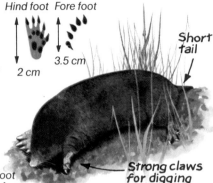

Hind foot   Fore foot

2 cm   3.5 cm

Short tail

Strong claws for digging

◀Hedgehog

Hedgerows, ditches, parks, gardens and moorland. Mainly nocturnal and lives on its own. Snuffles, squeals and snores. Rolls into a ball when alarmed. Eats animals like earthworms, frogs, slugs. H&B 25cm.

Hind foot   Fore foot

5 cm   4 cm

Prickles

Hair underneath

White-toothed Shrew ▶

Found on the Channel Islands, and the Isles of Scilly. Lives in hedges, gardens, edges of woods. Very active and mainly nocturnal. Eats earthworms, insects, spiders. H&B 8cm.

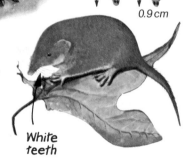

Fore foot   Hind foot

0.8 cm   0.9 cm

White teeth

Seals

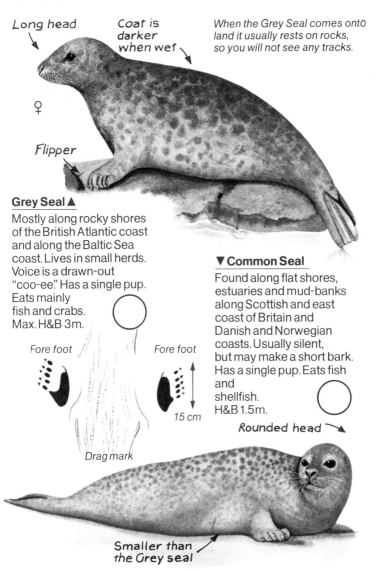

Long head

Coat is darker when wet

When the Grey Seal comes onto land it usually rests on rocks, so you will not see any tracks.

♀

Flipper

Grey Seal ▲

Mostly along rocky shores of the British Atlantic coast and along the Baltic Sea coast. Lives in small herds. Voice is a drawn-out "coo-ee." Has a single pup. Eats mainly fish and crabs. Max. H&B 3m.

▼ Common Seal

Found along flat shores, estuaries and mud-banks along Scottish and east coast of Britain and Danish and Norwegian coasts. Usually silent, but may make a short bark. Has a single pup. Eats fish and shellfish. H&B 1.5m.

Fore foot

Fore foot

15 cm

Drag mark

Rounded head ➤

Smaller than the Grey seal

Whales

These mammals are all whales and breathe air. They have a blow-hole on top of their heads for taking in air.

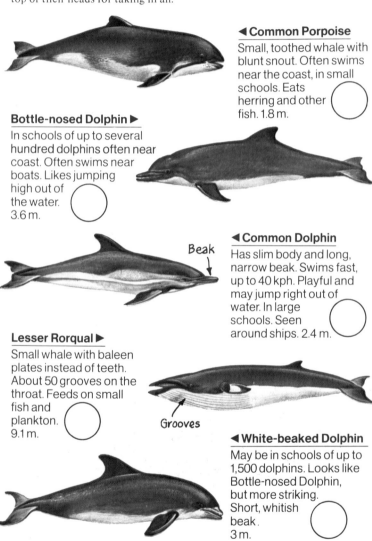

◄ Common Porpoise

Small, toothed whale with blunt snout. Often swims near the coast, in small schools. Eats herring and other fish. 1.8 m.

Bottle-nosed Dolphin ▶

In schools of up to several hundred dolphins often near coast. Often swims near boats. Likes jumping high out of the water. 3.6 m.

Beak

◄ Common Dolphin

Has slim body and long, narrow beak. Swims fast, up to 40 kph. Playful and may jump right out of water. In large schools. Seen around ships. 2.4 m.

Lesser Rorqual ▶

Small whale with baleen plates instead of teeth. About 50 grooves on the throat. Feeds on small fish and plankton. 9.1 m.

Grooves

◄ White-beaked Dolphin

May be in schools of up to 1,500 dolphins. Looks like Bottle-nosed Dolphin, but more striking. Short, whitish beak. 3 m.

Glossary

Abdomen - the hind section of an insect.

Algae - simple plants that range from minute plankton in the sea and in freshwater to large seaweeds.

Antenna (plural: antennae) - most insects have a pair of antennae (feelers) which they use for feeling and smelling.

Barbels - sensitive feelers. Fishes use their barbels to find their food on the bottom.

Breeding season - the time of year when a pair of animals mate and the females give birth and look after their young.

Camouflage - a colouring pattern that makes an animal difficult to see.

Carnivore - a meat eater Also the name of a large group of animals which includes bears, dogs, cats, weasels and their relatives. Most are meat eaters, but some, eg. bears, also eat plants.

Carrion - dead flesh. Some animals feed on the flesh of animals that have died or been left by carnivores.

Caste - social insects (eg. bees) consist of three castes (queens, drones and workers).

Chrysalis - see pupa.

Cocoon - a case which protects an insect pupa made by the larva before it pupates.

Colony - a group of animals living together.

Compound eye - an eye made up of many lenses.

Conifer wood - a wood made up of conifer trees which usually have narrow, needle-like, or scaly leaves, and produce seeds enclosed in cones.

Copse - a small wood, usually with lots of undergrowth.

Courtship display - when a male animal, especially a bird or fish, attracts a mate. Some show off their bright colours; others "dance" or put on a "display" in the air.

Cover - hedges, bushes, thick grass - anywhere that animals hide themselves.

Crown - the top of a bird's head.

Crustaceans - animals, such as crabs, prawns and shrimps, that have a hard shell.

Deciduous wood - a wood made up of trees which drop their leaves in autumn.

Den - the home of a fox.

Domestic animals - animals kept by man.

Drey - a squirrel's nest.

Drone - a male social insect.

Elytra (singular: elytron) - the wing covers of an insect (actually modified forewings).

Estuary - the mouth of a large river. Fresh water is mixed with sea water and at low tide large areas of mud are exposed.

Ewe - a female sheep.

Excrete - to get rid of waste from the body.

Extinct - a species of animals or plants that has completely died out.

Food plant - a plant that an animal species feeds on.

Fry - a young fish after the larval stage.

Gall - a swelling on a plant caused by an insect larva.

Game birds - ground-living birds, hunted by man eg. Pheasant.

Herbivore – an animal that feeds only on plants.
Hibernation – when animals sleep through most of the winter period. Their temperature falls and they eat nothing or very little.
Hind – a female Red Deer.
Honeydew – a sweet liquid excreted by some insects and eaten by others.
Host – an animal on which animals called parasites live and feed.

Insectivores – a group of animals which eat insects.

Juvenile – a young bird which has left the nest and whose plumage is not yet the same as its parents.

Lagomorphs – hares and rabbits.
Larva (plural: larvae) – the form which some animals take before they become adult, eg. the caterpillar form of a butterfly.
Lek – an area where male birds gather to display to females in the breeding season.
Lichen – small, dry-looking plants, rather like mosses.
Local – found only in certain areas.

Mammals – warm-blooded animals that usually have some hair on their bodies; the females give birth to live young which feed on the mother's milk.
Mermaid's purse – the egg case of a ray or dogfish.
Metamorphosis – the process of changing from an egg to an adult, via a larva and (often) a pupa.
Middle reaches – the portion of a river between the fast-flowing mountainous and the slow-flowing lowland portions.
Midwater – the water between the surface and the bottom of the sea.

Migration – the journey of certain animals from one area or country to another. Migrating animals are called **migrants.**
Mimicry – when an animal's shape or colour copies that of another species, or the plant it lives on.
Molluscs – animals, such as mussels and squids, that have a soft body, often protected by an outer shell.
Moult – when animals shed their hair or feathers and grow new ones. All birds shed their feathers at least once a year. In ducks, the duller plumage that remains after moulting is called **eclipse** plumage.

Nectar – a sweet-tasting liquid produced by flowers. Many insects feed on nectar.
Nocturnal – active mostly at night.
Nymph – the larva of an insect that does not pass through a pupal stage.

Omnivore – an animal that eats anything.
Order – one of the scientific divisions of animals (eg. the order Diptera includes all true flies).
Ovipositor – a female insect's egg-laying organ.

Parasite – an animal or plant that lives off the body of another animal or plant without giving anything in return.
Plankton – microscopic plants and animals that drift in water.
Plumage – a bird's feathers.
Predator – an animal that kills and eats other animals.
Prey – an animal that is hunted by another animal.
Proboscis – the long, tube-like "tongue" of some insects.

Pupa (plural: pupae) – the stage in an insect's life after the larval stage. The adult insect develops inside the pupa.

Queen – a female social insect which can lay eggs.

Reflex-bleeding – when an insect produces a liquid that looks like blood to frighten the enemy.
Rodents – a group of animals with long teeth for gnawing, eg. mice.
Roost – to sleep. A roost is a place where birds sleep.
Rump – the lower back and base of the tail of a bird.
Rut – the mating period of deer and other hoofed animals.

Scale-insect – a small, plant-sucking insect.
School – a group of fishes of the same species that swim together.
Set – the home of a badger.
Secrete – when an insect's body produces and gives off a chemical from a gland.
Social insects – insects that live in colonies and are organized so that each of three castes have different duties.

Solitary – living alone.
Spawn – to breed.
Species – a group of plants or animals that can reproduce with each other.
Stag – a male deer.

Territory – some animals defend part of the area in which they live; this is their territory.
Thorax – the middle section of an insect to which the legs and wings are attached.
Tundra – the cold, treeless area in the Arctic.

Ungulate – a hoofed mammal.

Vegetarian – a plant-eating animal.
Venomous – capable of injecting a venom by means of a bite or sting.
Visitor – see **Migrant.**
Worker – a female social insect that cannot breed. These insects work for the colony.

Index

This index gives the common English name of each species **in bold type,** followed by its Latin name *(in italics).*

Some species have more than one English name and so you will find that some entries refer you to an alternative name. For example, **Common Amaranth** is also known as **Pigweed**: if you look it up under **"Amaranth, Common",** the entry says *"see Pigweed",* the more common of the names for this species.

Some species are listed under more general headings. For example, all the butterflies are listed under **Butterfly,** followed immediately by

the individual species of butterflies in the book. All the different types of crickets are listed under **Cricket,** and so on.

If you look up a species name, you may find that the entry cross-refers to one of these general headings. For example, the entry **Ischnura, Common** says *"see under* Damselfly", since there are several types of damselfly, of which the Common Ischnura is one. This type of cross-reference has been included to help you in cases where it may not be obvious which general category a species belongs to.